Leave The Capital
A History Of Manchester Music In 13 Recordings

Paul Hanley

[signature: Paul Cully]

route

Published by Route
PO Box 167, Pontefract, WF8 4WW
info@route-online.com
www.route-online.com

ISBN : 978-1901927-71-9

Cover Design:
GOLDEN
www.wearegolden.co.uk

Printed in EU by Pulsio SARL

Contents

To Julie, for a groovy kind of love.

'Look Through Any Window'
The Hollies

'Bus Stop'
The Hollies

'No Milk Today'
Herman's Hermits

'East West'
Herman's Hermits

'A Groovy Kind Of Love'
The Mindbenders

'Matchstalk Men And Matchstalk Cats And Dogs'
Brian and Michael

'I'm Not In Love'
10cc

'Everybody's Happy Nowadays'
Buzzcocks

Unknown Pleasures
Joy Division

'Bankrobber'
The Clash

Perverted By Language
The Fall

The Smiths
The Smiths

'So Young'
The Stone Roses

Introduction

On 24th June 1929, 250 excited children from all ends of Manchester didn't go to school. Instead they packed their lunches in bread wrappers, kissed their mums goodbye, boarded buses and trams, and travelled into the city. Later that day, the Free Trade Hall, a grand Italianate civic hall built on the site of the infamous Peterloo Massacre, would witness a significant milestone in the history of Manchester music.

The Manchester Children's Choir was a diverse ensemble gathered from 52 of the city's elementary schools – it was assumed that grammar school children would be too busy with their studies to commit to the necessary practise. They had given many concerts and performances since their formation four years previously, but on this day they were shepherded together to make a musical recording with the Hallé Orchestra under the direction of the wonderfully named Sir Hamilton Harty.

The Hallé was a well-respected, professional body who had been making classical music accessible to Mancunians since 1858. Having their music recorded was a challenging experience for the otherwise jaded players of the orchestra, and most unusual – they didn't release a record of their own until years later. So this must have been a daunting prospect indeed for the school children. After all, practically no one made records, certainly not working-class Mancunian kids. Records were made by dinner-jacketed dance bands in America or London, two distant places many of them would never see. Before they entered the Free Trade Hall, the children could never have dreamed that they would record music that would touch people's hearts the world over.

The song the Manchester Children's Choir gifted to posterity wasn't particularly appropriate, as it happens. Purcell's 'Nymphs And Shepherds' was a slushy 200-year-old ballad about the joys of rural living, but it didn't matter. The combined voices of urban Manchester's offspring were so seductive that the record went on to sell a million copies. It was released by Columbia Records and was the UK's first significant recording outside of the capital. The whole episode was so delightfully Mancunian it was later the subject of a musical by Morrissey's favourite, the much-missed Victoria Wood.

The Free Trade Hall witnessed another milestone in music history when Bob Dylan's legendary move to electric guitar was captured for posterity in 1966. But it would be a full forty years after 'Nymphs And Shepherds' before anything else of significance was professionally committed to tape in Manchester.

The city wasn't alone in this of course. The Beatles managed to record an album's worth of songs in Hamburg as early as 1961, but didn't enter a professional recording studio north of Watford Gap in the whole of their career. 'Penny Lane', 'Strawberry Fields Forever', even The Pacemakers' 'Ferry Cross The Mersey' – all beautiful evocations of Liverpool life, all committed to tape in London. In fact, all of the North West bands that made it big in the early sixties recorded in London, there was simply nowhere else it could be done.

In the eyes of the world, the various bands of the Liverpool and Manchester beat boom were often lumped together, but the perennial rivalry that exists between those two fine cities meant it wasn't long before inter-city comparisons were made. After all, said rivalry has been a key driving force of every other cultural and technological phenomenon in the two cities since the industrial revolution. At its best this reciprocal chest-pounding has spurred the cities to such dazzling creativity as the Manchester Ship Canal, while at its worst it's spawned hideous football chants that exploit the most tragic of human suffering.

After the dust settled on the 'British invasion' of the sixties, attempts to weigh up which city had the most impact on the world have been inevitably skewed by the peerless influence of The Beatles. Mancunian music fans will argue that, the Fab Four aside, the rest of Liverpool's beat groups weren't quite as accomplished as the best Manchester had to offer. This argument obviously gets little traction on Merseyside; for North West residents such discussions will inevitably be coloured by which end of the East Lancs Road they live at.

It's much easier to quantify the effect this musical explosion had on the musical heritage of the cities themselves. If it is measured in terms of the financial and artistic riches the beat boom gave back to the city that birthed it, Manchester wins hands down. Because, significantly, it was four Mancunian musicians who first became alive to the possibility of recording away from the capital. With absolutely no guarantee of success, they opted to plough their hard-earned cash back into the city they loved in the form of proper recording facilities. In this they differed from most of their contemporaries – Mancs and Scousers alike. Despite waxing lyrical about the places they loved, most invested in nothing more than a one-way ticket to Euston and barely stopped to shake the dust from their brand-new Chelsea boots on the way.

By sheer force of will, Eric Stewart of The Mindbenders and songwriter extraordinaire Graham Gouldman created Strawberry Studios; Keith Hopwood and Derek Leckenby of Herman's Hermits crafted Pluto. Between them they paved the way for a dynasty that would be defined by its rejection of the capital. By providing facilities which could be accessed by cash-strapped Mancunians without the wherewithal to decamp to London, it was the studio owners of Manchester who facilitated a musical revolution. A revolution that once again began at the Free Trade Hall.

This is the story of how records were made in Manchester, back when studios mattered. This is the story of music that couldn't have been made anywhere else but Manchester.*

* For the purposes of this book, unless otherwise specified, the designation 'Manchester' refers to Greater Manchester, which covers the city and its outlying districts. Thus Stockport is 'in' Manchester, despite being a town in its own right. This means, of course, that Salford is in Manchester too, a delineation which has been the root of some disquiet amongst Salfordians over the years. But, with apologies to my friends in the west, the distinction between Manchester and Salford begins to fade by the time you get to Warrington, and means practically nothing to the rest of the world. Even some of what we now think of as Manchester city centre is technically in Salford, and any attempts to distinguish between the two in terms of musical history quickly becomes an exercise in nit-picking. So 'Manchester' it is.

'Why had those early Factory releases had that magical Hannett sound? The young genius had been able to plug in his digital thingy into the outboard racks of a major world-class thirty-six track studio that was in Stockport – Stockport ladies and gentleman, Stockport, because 10cc were a Manchester band and they had taken the proceeds of the delicious "I'm Not In Love" and had reinvested in their home. Reinvested. Built a fuck-off studio. Respect.'

– Tony Wilson (2002)

'Above all – remember – you're not Britain; you're Manchester.'

– Herman Tulley (1968)

PART I
The Way The
Whole Thing Started

Chapter 1
The Time Is Right

From Manchester To Manchester Square

In 1955, Glaswegian Lonnie Donegan unexpectedly reached the Top 10 in the UK with his version of 'Rock Island Line', an old American prison song first recorded in 1934, a mere five years after 'Nymphs And Shepherds'. But Donegan's version was as far away from dreamy pastoral sung in Received Pronunciation as it's possible to be, and it spoke to a new generation. The USA had recently invented the teenager: young people with money in their pockets who were in no rush to become their parents and, despite the fact that British teenagers were significantly less financially independent than their US counterparts, the phenomenon quickly spread across the Atlantic. For this nascent social group, America represented the Promised Land. They had already glimpsed the USA through films and comic books brought over by the American troops stationed in the UK and were about to experience arguably America's greatest gift to the world: rock and roll.

'Rock Around The Clock' broke big that same year. It was first heard in the film *Blackboard Jungle*, and it gave birth to Teddy Boys, juvenile delinquency and the generation gap overnight. The youth of Britain adopted Bill Haley as the harbinger of a new era of cool right up until the moment they encountered Elvis Presley, then they recognised the Comets for the over-the-hill kiss-curled wannabes they really were. Elvis, Little Richard, Chuck and Jerry Lee were the real deal, and it didn't take the terrified suits of the UK record industry long to notice. A lifetime before Simon Cowell, the money men realised that hand-picked, home-grown and compliant talent who could get the kids screaming but leave the cinema seats intact were the way to real fortunes. Turning rebellion into money became an industry in its own right.

The moguls had no inclination to scour the country in their quest to find these new stars. Manchester? You might as well have suggested Reykjavik. In truth they didn't really need to, as they had higher priorities than talent. The whole of the music industry was based in London so they simply walked from their offices in Denmark Street down Old Compton Street to Soho's 2i's Coffee Bar. They sat down, ordered their frothy coffees and signed up any frothy personality who was willing to give it a go. (They all took their coffee white of course. There were to be no British analogues for Little Richard or Chuck Berry.) Kids who had hopped on the tube to the Soho scene from nearby Bermondsey and Blackheath were locked into contracts, groomed for stardom and given new names, all with the suitably macho connotations that became *de rigueur*. Or nearly all anyway. When he heard his mates had been re-christened 'Cliff', 'Wilde' and 'Steele' respectively, Charlie Harris was understandably disappointed with his slightly less virile rebrand: 'Wee Willie'.

These toothsome troubadours ticked enough boxes to dominate the charts for several years, but away from the capital it didn't take long for the young working-class men of the North who'd fallen for Elvis *et al* to see right through the corporate cockney stooges. Taking their lead from the aforementioned Lonnie Donegan, they armed themselves with cheap guitars, tea-chest basses and washboards and strived to replicate the really important thing about the American acts: their attitude. By 1961 the grass root music scenes in Manchester and Liverpool had exploded and, because there were endless clubs and coffee bars to play, skiffle groups could earn enough to upgrade to real instruments. A grudging cross-border détente even allowed the best of the Manchester bands to play in Liverpool and vice versa, which if nothing else gave the young beatsters a chance to check out the opposition. To the young men in the midst of this scene it must have felt like everyone they knew was in a band, which was either a sobering or comforting thought, depending on how much faith they had in their own ability. Of course, the vast majority of this new wave of young talent was as willing to sell their souls for success as their predecessors in London. Most ended up similarly controlled and constricted but a select few had enough vision and drive to change the way the whole thing worked, forever.

*

On 4th May 1963 one such fledgling Manchester band had an audition for a major label at the Oasis Club on Lloyd Street. The Oasis was run by Ric Dixon, a giant on the Manchester scene. Dixon had gone from National Service to nightclub management via a job at the Co-operative Wholesale Society. As well as booking every important band in the country for the Oasis, he was also a director at Kennedy Street Enterprises. Kennedy Street was pretty much the only name in town as far as promotion was concerned and is a key part of any history of Manchester music. Founded by legendary impresario Danny Betesh, who'd started out as a humble ballroom manager, Kennedy Street represented pretty much every successful Manchester artist of the sixties. Certainly any Manc band that did anything in the US was on their books. Given their efficacy, the fact that the directors of Kennedy Street aren't as famous as Brian Epstein, Don Arden or Peter Grant is testament to how modest, professional and willing to put their artists first they were.

The singer heading to the Oasis for the audition that day was a young Glyn Ellis. While he may have lacked the vision of a Lennon or McCartney, he had drive to spare. By early 1963, the apprentice electrician from Levenshulme had graduated from skiffle to become an apprentice electric musician and was making a name for himself on the Manchester beat club scene. That name wasn't 'Glyn Ellis' of course; like most of his contemporaries he was completely in thrall to Americana and had decided he needed an appellation that proved it. While dreaming of the Mississippi on one of his Levy breaks, he came up with the perfect name by stealing the surnames of America's greatest cowboy and Elvis's drummer. A name that could easily have been torn from one of the Gary Cooper film posters he passed every day at The Regal: Wayne Fontana.

Wayne Fontana must have felt his chances were good as he moseyed into town on the 92 bus to meet his High Noon. His band, The Jets, had been playing regularly over the past three years and were as ready for the engagement as they could ever hope to be. What's more, the prospective label, a new subsidiary of Philips, was also named Fontana. How could they say no?

Unfortunately, Wayne lacked something else besides vision that May evening; of the four Jets, only bass player Bob Lang turned up. Whether it was nerves or a general disinclination to sign on the dotted line that made the rest of the Jets forsake him that day is a mystery, but it's unlikely they got lost; they'd played the Oasis at least twice in the previous six months. Whatever the reason, they picked a particularly inauspicious day to quit.

Wayne Fontana was not the kind of person to let a little matter like having no band come between him and stardom, and a quick appeal in the bar for musicians produced a suitable drummer and guitarist in short order. By coincidence, not only was Wayne auditioning for a label with the same name as him, the two musicians he drafted in were from a different band called The Jets.[1]

Eric Stewart, from Droylsden, was sitting at the venue's coffee bar with his bandmate Ric Rothwell when Wayne approached them. Eric was something of a veteran of the Manchester scene himself; he was also the guitarist for Jerry Lee and the Staggerlees despite the fact he'd only turned 18 that January.[2] He'd bought his first guitar aged 14, without much enthusiasm, when he was forced to sell the item he really cared about – his air rifle. His neighbour, whose kitchen window had recently become collateral damage in Eric's war on the neighbourhood Comanches and Apaches, gave him a choice. Either he lost the gun, or something even more precious. 'He threatened to take my head off,' Eric recalled later, 'so I went to a second-hand shop on National Road in Manchester and swapped the air rifle for a really battered old acoustic guitar.' Showing far more flair for his new instrument than he ever did as a gunslinger, Eric was good enough to be playing regular paying gigs within two years.

There was an all-pervasive wisdom surrounding auditions in the early years of the 1960s. It was felt that the most important thing to highlight to a record company was your crossover potential. As well as driving your young fans (who,

[1] This Jets centred on singer Barry James, whose stage name was the hardly more flamboyant Johnny Peters. You wouldn't bother, would you? In truth, the Manchester bands at that time, much like their rivals on Merseyside, seem to have swapped personnel as often as they swiped each other's material. It's possible that the two Jets were in fact different iterations of the same band, a band which saw various Hollies, Hermits and Dreamers pass through its ranks at one time or another.

[2] Jerry Lee was (surprise surprise) a stage name. The singer's real name was Charlie Barker, but he thought he'd avoid confusion with any similar sounding musicians by giving himself a new name. Makes sense.

after all, were the ones who would be buying your records) to a frenzy with your hippy hippy shake, the men in suits wanted to know that you could appeal to their mums and dads. Rock and roll was all very well, but it was for young people and they grew up all too quickly. If a label was going to invest in an act, they knew versatility and variety were more easily monetised than authenticity and attitude. Any act worth its salt needed to be able to tackle a waltz or a foxtrot as well as a twist.

This meant that The Beatles, four pill-popping, hard-drinking, working-class lads with a fearsome live set (which they'd honed to perfection in the roughest bars in Hamburg), chose to include such whimsical fare as 'The Sheik Of Araby', 'Till There Was You' and 'Bésame Mucho' in their failed audition for Decca. It also informed the songs Wayne directed Eric and Ric to play that evening. As well as asking his new recruits to master 'My Girl Josephine' by Fats Domino and Chuck Berry's 'Johnny B. Goode' (which every band in the country was doing), he commanded that they get their collective heads round 'Zip-A-Dee-Doo-Dah'.

Originally from the 1946 Disney film *Song of the South*, the track had recently re-entered the public consciousness via Bob B. Soxx's Phil Spector-produced single. Not that Eric Stewart minded this choice – the new version had enervated a whole generation of would-be lead players. During its recording, an accidentally-overloaded microphone on the amp meant that the guitar solo came out 'fuzzy' – an effect that Spector adored and practically every electric guitarist was striving for within the year. It was such a seductive sound that it directly led to the invention of the fuzzbox foot pedal, as memorably heard on 'Satisfaction'.

By all accounts the audition sounded like what it was – an

unrehearsed jam with unfamiliar musicians. Eric and Ric played the gig, wished Wayne all the best, and departed for the coffee bar thinking no more about it. They hardly had a chance to order their drinks before they were accosted by a clearly distracted Wayne Fontana. The erstwhile Glyn Ellis bubbled like the espresso machine behind him. 'Jack Baverstock, the guy from Philips, wants to give me a recording contract. But he wants the guys who were on stage with me. Do you want to join my group?'

The two musicians wryly noted that Wayne had wasted no time in making sure they knew who was boss, but so what? If it meant having a recording contract, Eric and Ric weren't going to hang about either. They were in, with one condition. They couldn't really leave The Jets to join The Jets, so a new name was required. Eric suggested 'The Mindbenders' in reference to a film poster he'd just seen advertising Dirk Bogarde's 1963 'psycho brainwashing thriller' of the same name. With Ric Dixon on board as their manager, the band began working on songs for their first single.

★

On Bank Holiday Monday, 5th August 1963, a momentous concert took place in a tatty, hastily-erected marquee on Abbotsfield Park, Urmston. The Beatles were reluctantly honouring a booking that was made before they broke big. They'd had a good time when they played the Urmston Show in 1962, met some nice people and enjoyed a couple of pints in the Bird In Hand, so they happily agreed to come back the following year. Things were a little different by then though – at the time of the second gig 'Please Please Me' was riding high, they were ready to release 'She Loves You' and they had made their final appearance at The Cavern two days before. It was clear their days of playing council functions in rundown suburbs were over. Brian Epstein had tried to wriggle out of the gig on safety grounds, citing the uncontrollable numbers the newly-famous Beatles could generate, but Urmston Council were having none of it. There was no way they were going to cancel their flagship festivities on the grounds they might be too successful.

The lads got changed in a shed on the nearby allotments and were smuggled into the venue in a Parks & Gardens van. Depending on who you ask, between 1,000 and 4,000 people braved the horrendous rain to catch a glimpse of the zeitgeist blowing through their backyard. The council had expected 12,000.

Davyhulme mates Peter Noone and Alan Wrigley had wandered along to Abbotsfield Park ostensibly to see The Tremeloes. They were in a band themselves, The Heartbeats. Peter had a nice voice, a winning smile and a stage name he was proud of, Peter Novac; Alan had been practising hard on his hire-purchase bass guitar, and they figured they had what it took to make it big. However, what they saw that day changed everything. Alan was (un)lucky enough to witness four astonishing musicians at a point in their career when a serious case could be made for them being the most experienced live act in the world. The Beatles had played nearly a thousand hours in Hamburg and a year of lunchtime gigs at The Cavern on their journey to Urmston, and it showed. Pete and Alan had seen plenty of bands live — good bands, with talented musicians – but they'd never seen anything like this. And that bass player! Not only was he technically better at his instrument than Wrigley could ever hope to be, he was, as Ian MacDonald has memorably pointed out, perfectly capable of 'singing, whilst simultaneously playing a bass-line in quavers. And winking at the girls in the front row.' Alan knew the game was up. 'We're fucked,' was just about all he could find to say on the subject, so he said it several times. His companion couldn't manage such heady levels of discourse and remained speechless throughout.

Peter was something of a showbiz kid, he'd been on TV several times – including a stint as Len Fairclough's son on *Coronation Street* – but in terms of charisma and sheer professionalism, this was beyond anything he'd ever imagined. He knew he'd never be able to compete with The Beatles at rock and roll, but then Paul took centre stage and sang 'Till There Was You'; the one they half-heartedly wheeled out when they needed to broaden their appeal, just as they had done for Decca, just as they would do for The Royal Variety and Ed Sullivan. John and George always struggled to take the song seriously, and Paul could only carry it off by covering himself with a self-conscious smirk, but it was clear the song went down a treat with the mums and dads. (And, more importantly, the girls, Peter noted.) Suddenly, Peter could see a way forward. He'd never do authentic Little Richard like Paul McCartney, but he could sing that syrupy stuff like he really meant it. He would do the kind of songs The Beatles were desperate to drop. Of course, to do those numbers justice he'd need proper musicians, so it was a good job Alan had decided that he wasn't good enough. It would save Peter a task later on.

In a matter of months, his plans for world domination began to take shape. The band were re-christened 'Hermits' and Peter was officially re-christened 'Herman', his nickname at the time. More importantly, the band headhunted a properly talented guitarist, Keith Hopwood, from The Falcons. Keith was an Urmston lad who was reluctantly persuaded to join the Hermits despite some serious reservations about their musical ability. He'd seen the band at Altrincham Stamford Hall and was less than enthralled. 'A cacophony of echo,' was the kindest thing he could find to say when pushed for an opinion. What did impress him was the serious amount of bookings the band had lined up as they were averaging four or five paying gigs a week. So, reasoning that it would be easier to fill in the gaps in the Hermits' musical ability than the ones in his old band's diary, he jumped ship.

The reason the Hermits were so busy was because another key person had arrived in Pete's life, a proper bona fide manager; someone who would become a crucial element in the success of the Manchester scene, Harvey Lisberg. Quite by chance, in autumn 1963, trainee accountant Lisberg attended a Heartbeats gig at a church hall in Davyhulme. Showing the foresight he eventually became famous for, he took on the band's managerial duties soon after. By early 1964, he'd instigated a series of deft executive decisions, and set about securing them a record deal. But when he finally got a reluctant Mickie Most[3] to listen to their demo he was informed in no uncertain terms that they would never be signed with their current line-up. Taking his cue from this – as Most hadn't actually said no – and sensing that this could be his last chance, he made the necessary changes in personnel. Alan Wrigley was, as he'd predicted the previous August, unceremoniously out on his arse, along with drummer Steve Titterington. Derek Leckenby and Barry Whitwam from fellow Manchester band The Wailers

[3] Most had been one of the artists discovered in the 2i's, where he worked as a singing waiter. He had a brief career as a pop star in South Africa with The Playboys before returning to the UK in 1962 to concentrate on A&R and production.

were brought in on guitar and drums respectively. The three-piece Wailers were originally going to be completely subsumed into the Hermits, but bass player Ian Waller got cold feet, necessitating Hermits rhythm guitarist, Karl Green, move to bass. This new line-up was a revelation and within three days they were good enough to be recorded for Radio Luxembourg at The Cavern in Liverpool.

Although picked for their ability rather than because they were mates, this upgrading of the line-up was done without direct record company interference, which wasn't the case with many of their contemporaries. These weren't distant session musicians either; the new players were South Manchester lads like the rest of the band. Lisberg really believed in the group and now they were ready, he put his money where his mouth was. He wanted Mickie Most to see them on their home turf and knowing the producer had a pronounced aversion to spending time north of Barnet, Lisberg made sure his trip was as painless as possible. He paid for Most's first-class return airfare to Manchester and a night in the Midland Hotel. This meant Most could catch a Hermits gig at the Beachcomber in Bolton, where they were always guaranteed an appreciative crowd, and be back in W1 by the next day. Mickie was convinced, as much by Lisberg's faith in his charges and Peter's resemblance to a young JFK as by their talent, and told the band he had a song for them to record. Piling into Harvey's mother's Ford Prefect, which was, rather ostentatiously for 1964, fitted with a record deck, the band were treated to their first listen to the song that would change their lives.

The Hermits' first single for EMI/Columbia was the Gerry Goffin and Carole King composition 'I'm Into Something Good', previously released by Earl-Jean McCrea of The

Cookies.[4] Like every other act in the country, they were forced to record in London, but signing to Mickie Most's production company rather than directly to EMI meant they didn't record at Abbey Road. Instead, they made their way to the slightly less prodigious Kingsway Studios in Holborn.[5] The band drove down from Manchester overnight and started recording at 11am. By 1pm, having committed both sides to tape, they were enjoying an overpriced flat pint in Leicester Square. They were back in Manchester by the end of the same day, having no more desire to spend time in the capital than Mickie Most did out of it.

The main thing the Hermits added to the original song, besides a significantly clearer production, was some double time handclaps, which not only gave the single its trademark bounce, but also provided a distinctive visual hook for Peter whenever he performed the song on TV, which, as it turned out, was quite a lot. The sheer infectiousness of 'I'm Into Something Good's feel-good bubblegum meant that it was a while before Herman's Hermits needed to make the trek to London to record a follow-up. It entered the charts at the end of August 1964 and spent 14 weeks in the Top 40, with two weeks at No. 1. It also showed up five times on *Top of the Pops*. As they weren't touring, and because at that time *Top of the Pops* was recorded at Rusholme in South Manchester, this meant that the band could spend most of their time in their hometown. The fact that the BBC's flagship, soon-to-be-world-renowned music programme was filmed in a

[4] The Cookies were backing singers for Little Eva ('The Locomotion') and also recorded Goffin & King's S&M favourite 'Chains' which The Beatles had included on their first album.

[5] Many bands recorded at Kingsway (also known as De Lane Lea). It was significantly upgraded as the sixties progressed. Acts who recorded there include the Rolling Stones, The Animals and Jimi Hendrix.

disused Wesleyan church on Dickenson Road, and not in their state-of the-art studios in London, will tell you all you need to know about the upper echelons of the BBC in 1964, and their attitude to pop music.

Despite the massive success of 'I'm Into Something Good', Harvey Lisberg was fully aware that the Hermits needed unique material – he even co-wrote the B-side 'Your Hand In Mine' with his business partner Charles Silverman. He was shrewd enough to realise that what the band really needed was a source of songs that weren't provided by Mickie Most, who clearly had enough power over them as it was. As fate would have it, his next managerial signing would provide Herman's Hermits with just the writer they needed, a composer every bit the equal of Goffin and King, and who, crucially for this story, was as Manc as the Hermits themselves.

★

Formed on the other side of town from Herman's Hermits, The Whirlwinds were a six-piece who began their career as the resident showband for the Jewish Alliance Brigade's youth night. They went down a storm and their precocious young guitarist, Graham Gouldman, soon realised they needed to spread their wings. He approached his dad's friend, their neighbour Harvey Lisberg, and asked him to manage the band. Harvey was far too busy with the Hermits to take on another beat group, but to get Graham off his back he secured them some gigs in central Manchester, mainly at the Oasis and the legendary Twisted Wheel.

Graham Gouldman, from Broughton in Salford, had turned to guitar when he was 11 after a brief flirtation with drums. His first guitar was a cheap acoustic his cousin had bought him back from Spain, more as a souvenir than as a

31

suggestion for a hobby, but for Graham it was love at first sight. He gave up all other ambitions on the spot, left school as soon as it was legally possible and formed The Whirlwinds not long after that. Desperate to prove he was a serious musician, Gouldman's first move was to invest a not inconsiderable sum in a striking red Fender Stratocaster. Strats went for about £100 in the early sixties, so this was some serious outlay given that the average yearly wage was around £800. Such a prestige instrument set him above his contemporaries and the lesser bands who played at the youth nights – like The Sabres, who featured his friends Kevin Godley and Laurence Creme – could only look on in envy.

In fact all The Whirlwinds invested time and money in their act; by the time they were playing the bigger Manchester nightspots they had matching suits and matching dance moves. They must have felt all their hard work and investment had paid off when they secured a deal with the HMV Pop label. As it turned out, HMV would only stump up for a one-off single, which they insisted was a cover of Buddy Holly's thoroughly unexceptional 'Look At Me'. The only vaguely interesting thing about the original was that it was piano led rather than featuring Buddy's trademark guitar, so naturally the first thing The Whirlwinds did when they made the inevitable trip to London (the single was recorded in Abbey Road Studio 3) was to rearrange it for guitar and top it with a particularly bonkers guitar solo.

Given his impending position as the go-to writer for Manchester bands looking to find a hit, it's surprising that Graham was not confident enough in his songwriting ability to pitch a number to HMV, even for the B-side. Instead, The Whirlwinds somehow ended up recording Lol Creme's 'Baby Not Like You' – which was presumably deemed suitable because its intro featured the exact same two chords as 'Look At Me' played in the identical rhythm and tempo. Graham's solo on this side was diverting though, and by far the standout element of a sub-Merseybeat potboiler. The single was the kind of thing the Fab Four, beavering away in Studio 2 next door, were already light years beyond. It tanked, and Graham disbanded The Whirlwinds within the year.

Convinced he could do at least as good a job as Lol had done, Gouldman worked hard on improving his own material and decided to put together a new band, The Mockingbirds, in order to showcase it. Joining him from The Whirlwinds were the guitarist Stephen Jacobson, and the bassist who, in a marvellous example of nominative determinism, was called Bernard Basso. Gouldman stole The Sabres' drummer, his pal Kevin Godley, to complete the line-up. When the prospect of a deal with Columbia materialised, Graham was determined that one of his songs would be the first single.

On his lunchbreak in the fitting room of Bargains Unlimited, the Salford gent's outfitters where he worked, he wrote two tracks for his new band's first release. Quickly proving he had what it took to be a major songwriter, he created the genuinely innovative 'For Your Love' by simply pilfering the chords from 'House Of The Rising Sun' and changing the rhythm. At that time every guitarist in the country was ripping off 'House Of The Rising Sun' so it's a mark of Gouldman's innate talent that 'For Your Love' has endured as long as its progenitor. Even as he turned the shop sign back from 'Closed' to 'Open', Gouldman knew he had a hit on his hands. Which is more than Columbia did because they preferred his other offering, 'That's How It's Gonna Stay', for the A-side. Determined not to waste 'For Your Love' as a B-side, Gouldman came up with the distinctly

Beatlesesque 'I Never Should've Kissed You' virtually on the spot. It was frustrating, to say the least. What he needed was someone to champion his songs and give them the push they needed. For that he turned once again to Harvey Lisberg.

Lisberg was something of a visionary. With very little evidence, he recognised that Graham had a talent that would take him beyond The Mockingbirds and cement both their places in Manchester music history. He was convinced that 'For Your Love' was a potential hit and, more importantly, that there would be more where that came from. He encouraged Graham to work at his songwriting by placing him on a small retainer while he began to hone his skills. Thus doing, Lisberg created the conditions whereby Manchester bands that couldn't write their own hits could still boast a writer with the same background, experience and mindset as them.

That said, the first song his new manager successfully placed for Gouldman wasn't given to a Manchester band at all. Such was his belief in the merits of 'For Your Love', Harvey Lisberg suggested the song should be pitched to The Beatles. Gouldman wasted no time in reminding him that The Beatles weren't doing too badly in the songwriting stakes themselves and urged him to reconsider. However, Lisberg was so sure this was a good idea that at one of The Beatles' Hammersmith Odeon gigs in December 1964, he foisted The Mockingbirds' unreleased version of the song on publisher Ronnie Beck and asked him to get it to the Fab Four. Unsurprisingly, Beck chickened out of bothering the headline act with a song they neither wanted nor needed. Instead, much to Lisberg's annoyance, he played it to the support band, The Yardbirds. The Yardbirds and their manager, Giorgio Gomelsky, obviously had a better idea of what constitutes a hit than Columbia did and pounced on the song, recording it within the month.[6] Ironically, they were also signed to the Columbia label but presumably had a little more clout than The Mockingbirds and were able to force the cloth-eared label bosses to release it.

The song was a pop classic, its effortless appeal belying the patience, craft and talent that created it, and it went Top 10 in the UK and the US. The Yardbirds retained the signature bongo riff, as played by The Mockingbirds' guitarist Stephen Jacobson on the original, but added a brilliant harpsichord part, played by session maestro Brian Auger.[7] Their guitarist, Eric Clapton, was so horrified by the song's obvious allure that he left the group before it was released. Like many of his contemporaries, Clapton was a musical purist (or 'snob' for short) who scorned the notion of 'pop' and felt that the blues was the only truly authentic musical form. He presumably considered blues the most appropriate vehicle to convey the considerable angst and suffering of middle-class white boys from the stockbroker-belt. He also believed, far from uniquely, that authenticity and mass appeal were mutually exclusive.

Despite the fact that they now had a successful songwriter, The Mockingbirds struggled to gain a foothold in the charts themselves. This was possibly exacerbated by their refusal to move to London. Though being one of the few bands still based in Manchester who knew their way around a studio,

[6] It was recorded in London, at IBC Studios on 5th January 1965.

[7] Auger played Hammond organ on many classic sixties recordings and had previously been a member of Long John Baldry's Steampacket with Julie Driscoll and Rod Stewart. He insists the reason the part was played on the in-house harpsichord was because the group had forgotten to hire in a Hammond, but as it fits the song like a glove, and the studio was more likely to have an organ onsite than a harpsichord anyway, this is probably an urban myth.

it did allow them to secure the gig as warm-up band for *Top of the Pops*.

On April Fools' Day 1965, Graham must have felt the joke was on him. He found himself in the slightly surreal position of watching The Yardbirds storm onto *Top of the Pops* and thence to No. 3 in the hit parade with the song he'd written and had rejected for The Mockingbirds. His band, by contrast, were packed up and in the bar well before the cameras were turned on.

★

While it was clear that the original Jets had done Wayne Fontana a massive favour by missing their audition, it would still be a while before he achieved his ambition to have hits on both sides of the Atlantic. Eric Stewart and Ric Rothwell were both top-class musicians with an instinctive grasp of the mechanics of recording and gelled with bassist Bob Lang like they'd been a unit for years. Despite their obvious capability and willingness to source material from anywhere and everywhere, the new band struggled to land their first hit. By May 1964, The Mindbenders had released four competent, but largely ignored, singles. These included the song they'd performed that fateful day at the Oasis, 'My Girl Josephine', re-christened 'Hello Josephine' to better reflect the lyric.[8] On the record they played 'Josephine' much faster and harder than Fats Domino's original, and did their level best to inject some zip into a run-of-the-mill twelve-bar blues. This included adding some deranged call-and-response 'Ha Ha Ha's either side of the guitar solo.[9] Sadly,

[8] Most versions of this song, from Jerry Lee Lewis to Shakin' Stevens, are listed as 'Hello Josephine'.

[9] Dutch-based Manchester band The Scorpions, who featured some of Wayne's original Jets, later had a massive hit in the Netherlands with 'Hello Josephine' in an arrangement largely based on The Mindbenders' version. It upped the manic

their efforts weren't enough to give them the break they needed, and The Mindbenders' next three singles didn't overly bother the charts either. It wasn't until they released the curiously named 'Um, Um, Um, Um, Um, Um'[10] that they finally got to break into the UK Top 10. This was another song that had previously been a hit in the US, written by no less a talent than Curtis Mayfield, though it was Major Lance, later to be a big name on the Northern soul scene, who took it to No. 5 in the Billboard Hot 100 in 1963.

Keeping the same basic arrangement, The Mindbenders stripped the song right back, removed the percussion and cleverly rearranged the brass parts for Spanish guitar. As well as emphasising the wistfulness of the lyric, this sparse instrumentation really helped the production. Everything, from the handclaps to Ric Rothwell's tinkling hi-hats, came out crystal clear. It took two attempts to get it sounding this good – the first version, produced by Andrew Loog Oldham, didn't meet Jack Baverstock's exacting standards so he had them re-record it and this time produced it himself. Eric Stewart insisted later that the two versions were near-identical, but as most of Oldham's contemporary productions for the Rolling Stones sound like they're dipped in sludge, this seems unlikely. 'Um, Um, Um, Um, Um, Um' was by far the best thing The Mindbenders had done, and its sales reflected the fact. It reached No. 5 in the UK charts and Wayne Fontana and the Mindbenders appeared on *Top of the Pops* four times before Christmas.

laughter even further and invented a short-lived musical style called 'Freakbeat' which foreshadowed the psychobilly of The Cramps by a dozen years. The Scorpions continued to be big on the revival circuit in the Netherlands until, while being treated at home in Denton for stomach cancer in 1985, their singer Peter Lewis became the youngest murder victim of 'Dr Death' Harold Shipman, aged just 42.

[10] The lyric is clearly 'Mm, Mm, Mm, Mm, Mmm'.

The fact that they finally had a hit under their belt meant that Fontana were agreeable to the idea of releasing a Mindbenders album. The band wasted no time and shuttled straight down to Philips Studio on Hyde Park Corner. As was the norm at the time, they recorded the whole thing in a day, with only a session pianist on hand to fill out the sound. It was mostly made up of the cover versions that formed their live act, the highlight of which was 'A Certain Girl', an Allen Toussaint rocker that The Yardbirds had previously recorded. Unsurprisingly, the drumming's much better on the Mindbenders' version, and of the two Erics, the guitar solo Eric Stewart produced is vastly more satisfying than Clapton's. The band managed to sneak one original song onto the album, the lovely 'One More Time'. Though this was an accomplished ballad written by Eric Stewart and Wayne Fontana, all in all the album was something of a throwaway. The Mindbenders' main priority at this stage was securing another hit single.

That hit duly came along in the shape of Clint Ballard Jr.'s 'The Game Of Love'. Ballard was a songwriter from El Paso, Texas, most of whose own recordings were released under the name Buddy Clinton. However, he found his songs achieved far greater success when they were farmed out to other artists than when he tried to keep them for himself. For a time he worked in the Brill Building in New York writing hits for Frankie Avalon and Frankie Lane and even co-writing with Burt Bacharach. In May '64, Merseybeat bandwagoners The Swinging Blue Jeans made the charts with his song 'You're No Good', a recent US hit that had done nothing in the UK. At that point he became, like Goffin and King, one of the go-to writers for British bands wishing to crack America; Jack Baverstock secured 'The Game Of Love' for his boys and Philips before anyone else could claim it.

The Mindbenders' recorded version is a revelation, and despite its distinctly heterocentric lyric, it's years ahead of its time. The drum intro is especially prescient, both in terms of EQ and execution – it was sampled wholesale by Eminem in 2013 for 'Love Game'. Furthermore, switching Ric Rothwell's whip-crack snare to a floor tom will give you the intro to 'Live Forever' by Oasis. The mid-song change to a Bo Diddley beat, which could easily jar in the hands of lesser musicians, feels completely natural, and the bass guitar and harmonies are fantastic. Bass harmonies were provided by Cliff Hall from Fontana label mates The Spinners[11] who had journeyed south to record next door (it wasn't even possible to record four blokes with two acoustic guitars outside London in 1965). Regent Sound Studios' guitarist-in-residence Jimmy Page was on hand to lend Eric his Les Paul, though his guitar playing skills were definitely not required, and the resulting lead is suitably impressive. What's more, the unusual double-time fade-out was copied a couple of months later by The Beatles on 'Ticket To Ride'. Its overall tone even presages the moody darkness of The Doors, who formed the year it was released. All in all, it's an incredibly soulful and well-crafted single which barely makes it past the two-minute mark. It reached No. 2 in the UK and went to No. 1 in the US just in time to coincide with The Mindbenders' first American tour. What could possibly go wrong?

★

Over in the Herman's Hermits camp, Mickie Most was similarly unconcerned with where material originated. As far

---

[11] The Spinners were a jocular loud-shirted North West folk group who were inexplicably never off the telly in the seventies. Motown's Spinners had to rebrand themselves 'The Detroit Spinners' in the UK to avoid confusion.

as he was concerned it was image that made a band unique, not songs, and he was in no rush to tamper with a winning formula. As a follow-up to 'I'm Into Something Good' he had Herman's Hermits record 'Show Me Girl', another Goffin and King number, for their second single. This time though, the Hermits, with the negotiating power that only a transatlantic hit can provide, got their hands on it first. As 'I'm Into Something Good' was taking longer to climb the charts in the US,[12] 'Show Me Girl' was only released in the UK. It was slightly more downbeat than its predecessor, but then again, most songs are. It also attempted to strike a more cautious note with its reassurance-seeking lyric and shift to a minor key for the bridge. Truth be told, it wasn't a patch on 'I'm Into Something Good' and consequently struggled to reach No. 19 at the end of November. Deciding that the public probably preferred the relentlessly happy-go-lucky version of the Hermits, Most had them issue a different follow-up in the US.

'Can't You Hear My Heartbeat' was, conversely, written by a British songwriting team, John Carter and Ken Lewis,[13] later of The Ivy League. Listening to it with hindsight, it's a much more obvious follow-up to 'I'm Into Something Good'. It's got its predecessor's double-time handclaps, it pinches John Lennon's ridiculously contagious triple-time chord work from 'All My Loving' for the solo,[14] and is blessed with a lyric so sunnily optimistic it makes 'I'm Into Something Good' sound

[12] It eventually reached No. 13 in December, selling a million copies in the process.

[13] Their band at the time, Carter-Lewis and the Southerners, boasted Jimmy Page on guitar. They were based in the Regent Sound recording studio on Denmark Street where The Mindbenders had recorded 'Um, Um, Um, Um, Um, Um'. Of course in 1964, any band based in a recording studio would have to be Southerners.

[14] Not that Lennon could complain – he'd filched it from 'Da Doo Ron Ron' by The Crystals.

like Leonard Cohen. Despite the fact it's not quite as good a song, 'Can't You Hear My Heartbeat' made No. 2 in the US, even higher than the previous single. It cemented the image of Herman and his Hermits as perennial purveyors of naive Northern (or in the US, English) charm in the minds of their fans forever. Mickie Most deliberately promoted Peter Noone, a working-class lad from Davyhulme, as a clean-cut preppy pop star in the mould of Bobby Vee, the better to differentiate the Hermits from the Rolling Stones. Of course The Stones' image as bad boys you couldn't introduce to your mother was as far removed from reality as Peter's was. Mick, Keith and Brian's polite middle-class Home Counties roots shone through in every interview they gave, at least until they learned to disguise their accents behind a pseudo-cockney speaking voice that was no more genuine than Mick's American singing.

With their second hit in the bag, Herman's Hermits were up and running. They made their first visit to the US at the end of December 1964, leaving their British fans with a stop-gap EP to remember them by.[15] This was a promotional trip rather than a tour and included the band's movie debut, when they were shoehorned into *When The Boys Meet The Girls*, a dismal musical starring Connie Francis. The film was something of a dog's breakfast, and it certainly covered as many musical bases as possible: the other artists who featured were Liberace, Louis Armstrong and Sam the Sham. It wasn't exactly high art, but the group got to dress as cowboys and sing two songs, one of which, 'Listen People', Harvey Lisberg had secured from Graham Gouldman. For the Hermits, the film was just another step on the ladder. All in all, the band's

---

[15] *Hermania*. It contained fairly lacklustre covers of songs that had previously been hits in the US by other artists.

trajectory was incredible, given that only 14 months earlier, Lisberg was watching them play a glorified youth club in Davyhulme.

Herman's Hermits' 1965 was frantic. They toured the UK in March on the back of their second UK Top 5 hit, 'Silhouettes'. April saw them play the New Musical Express Poll Winners Concert at the Empire Pool Wembley, and they toured North America for the first time in May. For three of the four weeks they were on tour, they were No. 1 in the US with 'Mrs Brown You've Got A Lovely Daughter'. The song was reluctantly extracted from their first album for US-only release when MGM, their US label, received 700,000 pre-orders for a single that didn't exist. Nobody in the band particularly liked the song, and nor did Mickie Most; it was only added to their first LP as an afterthought. It was the joke number the band used to play to leaven their R&B-heavy live set. Pete used to perform it wearing a school blazer and satchel, exploiting his loveable Manc little brother persona to the hilt. The threadbare opening guitar and the vocal mannerisms were deliberately reminiscent of that other North West working-class icon, George Formby, and Noone clearly relished the chance to pronounce such words as 'lovely' and 'enough' with a proper Manchester inflection.[16] Despite having a good time recording what they clearly regarded as a makeweight, the group were mortified when Most announced he was bowing to pressure and releasing it in the US as single; even he thought it was too gauche to be released in the UK. It was a colossal hit in America though, and it led

[16] When southern journalist types try to convey this pronunciation in print they invariably use a double 'o' – as in 'rook' – hence interviews with the Gallagher brothers filled with references to 'Fookin' Man City' and the like. This causes much confusion (and annoyance) to actual Mancunians, who normally read 'oo' as in 'loop'.

to them being as successful as The Beatles for a while. It was a two-edged sword of course, as it was this song more than any other that scuppered their chances of ever being taken seriously as a group. Still, they had five more US Top 10 hits that year,[17] including the ridiculous 'I'm Henry VIII I Am' which was even less credible than 'Mrs Brown', so no one was complaining too hard.

There was clearly a market in the US for novelty acts with a Manchester lilt – fellow Mancunians Freddie and the Dreamers made a killing with an act that made Herman's Hermits look positively restrained. It included ridiculous dance routines, maniacal cackling and the odd bit of trouser dropping, all centred on Crumpsall-born Freddie Garrity's loveable daftness. Renowned rock critic Lester Bangs rather unkindly called Freddie and the Dreamers 'a triumph of rock as cretinous swill'. Nonetheless, Garrity scored an impressive five Top 50 hits in the US, including a No. 1 with 'I'm Telling You Now'. This was the first of three consecutive US No. 1s by Manchester artists, the others being (of course) Herman's Hermits and Wayne Fontana and the Mindbenders. Take that Liverpool!

These three Manchester bands with the world at their feet were soon to be joined by a fourth, The Hollies, whose brilliant vocal harmony and assured musicianship would eclipse them all. But though they'd managed to match The Beatles in sales, none of them had achieved anything like the same cultural impact. Because they were beholden to professional songwriters from New York, LA and London,

[17] Including 'A Must To Avoid' which Pete liked to introduce onstage as 'A Muscular Boy'. By November 1965 they had enough material to fill their first greatest hits compilation, released a mere 15 months after their first single.

they inevitably spoke to the world in a voice that barely resembled their own. Luckily for them, a songwriter who had walked the same Manchester streets was about to compose some of the finest songs of his career. Of course, even Graham Gouldman wasn't prolific enough to write every single for The Hollies, Freddie and the Dreamers and The Mindbenders, and Mickie Most would take some convincing before he'd give Graham a crack at a Hermits A-side. However, he had enough of a presence in all their catalogues over the next few years to ensure Manchester bands could speak to the world with a coherent and authentic Mancunian voice. And speak to the world they did.

Chapter 2
Everybody's Got To Have Their Day

"For Your Love"–The Yardbirds
"No Milk Today"–Herman's Hermits
"Behind the Door"–Cher
"Pamela, Pamela"–Wayne Fontana
"Bus Stop"–The Hollies

These great hits have
one thing in common.
They were all written
by Graham Gouldman...

and now he makes
his Victor singing debut
with his newest song...
"THE IMPOSSIBLE YEARS"
c/w "No Milk Today" 9453

RCA

Graham Gouldman's Manchester Quadrilogy
Look Through Any Window
Bus Stop
No Milk Today
East West

Despite his obvious prowess as a songwriter, Graham Gouldman was unable to achieve success with The Mockingbirds. As a result he was regularly forced to traipse down to London to try to sell his songs to the various Denmark Street publishing houses like they were brushes or miracle cleaner. At the same time, and with no lack of irony, fellow Mancunians like Freddie and the Dreamers and The Hollies, who'd upped sticks and moved to London to be nearer the action, were often to be found visiting the same publishers to try and secure their next hit single.

Returning to Manchester with Graham on the train from one such song pitching expedition, Harvey Lisberg's business partner Charles Silverman asked the songwriter where he got his lyrical inspiration. Graham revealed that one method was to watch strangers go about their daily business and try to imagine the motivations that put them in that particular place. As they gazed out at the passing houses, Silverman was enthralled.

'So you could literally look through any window and come up with an idea?'

Gouldman was sufficiently grateful for this inspiration that the resulting song 'Look Through Any Window' was credited to Gouldman–Silverman. And like many of Graham Gouldman's best songs, its melancholic mood is distinctly Mancunian in outlook. Harvey Lisberg sensed as much and knew it should be given to a Manchester band, but try as he might be couldn't get Mickie Most to record the song with Herman's Hermits. As it was clear the song didn't have a sufficient daftness quotient to suit Freddie and the Dreamers, Lisberg instructed publisher Ronnie Beck to get the song to Manchester's other leading lights, The Hollies.

The story of The Hollies began with two Salford schoolmates who were stirred to start a band after watching a seminal gig at the Free Trade Hall on 22nd April 1960. Allan Clarke and Graham Nash were so impressed with The Everly Brothers performance that they immediately resolved to form a vocal duo of their own. They even followed the brothers back to the Midland Hotel and were delighted when Don and Phil were gracious enough to speak to them. The Everlys were generous with their time and amongst the general encouragement they passed on an important tip: make sure you write your own songs. That was good advice, but far easier said than done in those days, and The Everly Brothers knew it. Once they'd signed for Parlophone,[18] The Hollies' early recording sessions in Abbey Road followed a familiar, fairly uninspiring pattern. And no wonder! George Martin had ceded an unprecedented amount of control to The Beatles when he let them pick their own songs, let alone write them, and no one wanted that to catch on. A lot of people's lucrative careers at EMI were based on their supposed ability to match songs with the correct artiste, so the upcoming proliferation of self-contained bands would see many of them effectively out of a job.

Consequently, half of The Hollies first eight singles were re-runs of old songs. The rest were sourced from the tried-and-trusted list of American songwriters who sent their songs to the UK with no preference as to who recorded them. Legendary songsmith Mort Shuman gave them a single and,

[18] They'd been spotted by George Martin's assistant, Ron Richards, when they supported The Beatles at The Cavern.

somewhat inevitably, Manchester favourites Gerry Goffin and Clint Ballard Jr. contributed one each.

They did manage to sneak one of their songs onto an A-side, the genuinely eccentric 'We're Through'. However, it had so little going for it that it was probably sanctioned as a single to prove to the band that their management knew best. Although written by Clarke, Nash and guitarist Tony Hicks, it was credited to 'L. Ransford'. The band were told that 'Clarke–Nash–Hicks' was too long to be printed on the label, which seems disingenuous given that it's only one character longer than 'Lennon–McCartney'. It's more likely that Parlophone didn't want anyone to know that the band had started writing their own material.

They needn't have worried, it's a terrible song, clearly cobbled together by a band eager to show off their musical skills. It's built around the sort of riff that will sound familiar to anyone who's ever frequented a musical instrument shop and a vocal that features the kind of aimless melisma that would ruin many a good tune in the eighties.[19] It's further hampered by a dreadful overdubbed handclap on the one and three beats[20] and a lyric which was pretty trite even by 1965 standards.

Though it made it to No. 7 in the UK on the back of their previous hits, 'We're Through' was never going to give them the break in the US they needed. Their hopes of emulating fellow Mancs the Hermits on the other side of the pond

[19] Melisma is defined as 'the singing of a single syllable of text while moving between several different notes in succession'. A particularly galling example is Whitney Houston's grandiloquent version of Dolly Parton's delightful 'I Will Always Love You'. There's plenty of other examples to get vexed about, of course, my own particular bête noire being 'There Must Be An Angel' by Eurythmics.

[20] Basically the kind of clapping your mum does. Largely wiped out now but there's still the odd outbreak at weddings/The Royal Variety.

were fading fast, so when Ronnie Beck presented them with Graham Gouldman's impressive demo of 'Look Through Any Window', they must have been mightily relieved.

The Hollies recorded 'Look Through Any Window' at Abbey Road on the 30th June 1965, and it was everything its predecessor wasn't. A particularly satisfying and well-rounded song, the empathy of its bittersweet third-person storytelling predates Paul McCartney's similar shift in subject matter later the same year.[21] It certainly inspired a much better performance from the band, especially Bobby Elliott, whose drumming is hugely inventive throughout. The melody line and harmonies are appropriate in their restraint; the Byrds-like guitar riff remembers to be appealing as well as skilful and, thank the Lord, the handclaps are in the right place. Released in America in September, it saw them break into the Billboard Top 40 for the first time when it reached No. 32 in January 1966. This was real progress for the band, and proved once and for all that The Hollies, like all artists who record other people's material, do their most enduring work with songs that contain some personal resonance.

The marriage of The Hollies' musicianship and Graham Gouldman's songwriting skills was clearly a match made in heaven. But the seven-month gap between recording 'Look Through Any Window' and it hitting the Top 40 in the States, meant that the band had recorded singles by two other writers before returning to their fellow Mancunian.

The first of these was an ill-advised cover of 'If I Needed Someone', George Harrison's celebrated Byrds homage/lift. The Hollies recorded it within a month of The Beatles, under

---

[21] Throughout his career the ever-empathetic John Lennon remained scornful of songs he referred to as 'these stories about boring people doing boring things – being postmen and secretaries and writing home', despite (or more probably because of) the fact his partner was brilliant at them.

the mistaken belief that it was written especially for them. It would probably have been a good idea to check – they only had to nip next door, after all – because the claim was obviously untrue. The Beatles loved the song and were fully intent on releasing it themselves. In fact 'If I Needed Someone' holds a unique position in Beatles folklore as the only George Harrison song they ever performed live onstage. Embarrassingly for The Hollies, once it was released it was reported that Harrison 'detested' their version.[22] But even if George had sanctioned it, Manchester's finest releasing a Beatles song as a single on the same day as *Rubber Soul* came out was a terrible idea. Hollies bassist Eric Haydock likened it to 'running onto Manchester City's pitch wearing a United outfit' and he quit the band in disgust soon after. 'If I Needed Someone' limped to No. 20 in the UK and disappeared without trace in America. Embarrassed by the obvious gaffe, the band hastily released another single, this time a cover of Evie Sands's 'I Can't Let Go', but again failed to make the Top 40 in the US.

Graham Gouldman was still playing and recording with The Mockingbirds, but the chances of them securing a hit of their own were fading fast. They'd been signed to Andrew Loog Oldham's Immediate label, then Decca, releasing several singles which did absolutely nothing. Given that Gouldman was a talented songwriter and had boosted the band's profile with his hits for others,[23] it's hard to pinpoint exactly what The Mockingbirds were missing. It certainly wasn't ideas. In

[22] 'They've spoilt it. The Hollies are alright musically but the way they do their records they sound like session men who've just got together in a studio without ever seeing each other before.' (Quoted in *NME*.) He subsequently denied ever saying it, and blamed an unnamed PR person. (Yeah, right.)

[23] Gouldman's songs spent more time on the UK chart during 1965-1966 than anyone outside of The Beatles/Rolling Stones.

fact their long-forgotten single 'You Stole My Love' has too many ideas for its own good. It's built around a brilliant – and typically Mancunian – riff, half of which later turned up on Joy Division's 'Novelty'. It's such a good lick it's surprising no one's lifted it in its entirety – The Charlatans or The Stone Roses (or maybe The Fall then The Stone Roses) could definitely do something with it. The Mockingbirds themselves squandered it – just as the song establishes itself as a thumping garage tune there's an awkward shift into a waltz which kills the momentum stone dead.[24]

The Mockingbirds were definitely lacking a strong image, and the sound of their eclectic singles never really gelled into a coherent direction, but maybe the world just wasn't ready for them: 10cc would eventually take both these supposed drawbacks and turn them into their greatest strengths.

Luckily The Mockingbirds' live commitments gave Graham the opportunity to mix with acts who had a reasonable chance of turning his songs into hits. While supporting The Hollies at Stoke Town Hall he seized one such opportunity and presented the band with a follow-up to 'Look Through Any Window'. This one, he assured them, was written especially for them. And in the less-than-salubrious surroundings of the backstage toilets, Graham gifted The Hollies one of the best examples of his songwriting skills, and arguably their finest single.

'Bus Stop' is also one of his most Manchester-inspired tunes. You can tell that because it's a story that revolves around an umbrella and it's set in July. In actual fact the couple share the umbrella whether it's raining or not, much to their fellow passengers' confusion. Gouldman wrote the lyric while taking the bus home from South to North Manchester, and the

[24] When The Yardbirds tried covering the song they never made it past the tricky time change and had to abandon plans to record it.

inspirational quality of the journey held enough resonance for him that both the bus number and the route it took were permanently lodged in his memory.

'I began writing it whilst riding on the No. 95 bus which ran from East Didsbury – the route went through Manchester city centre, to Sedgley Park, Cheetham Hill, Prestwich, and on to Whitefield near Bury,' he told *Mojo* in 2011.

He also remembered the song as one of the few occasions where inspiration struck with little or no effort. That's not to say the song is simplistic – its internal rhymes and inventive phrasing remain thoroughly engaging throughout. Musically, the song's minor chord progressions and instrumental break are indebted to the traditional Jewish musical form Klezmer; all of which make the song such a satisfying reflection of Graham's life and personality. It's a shame he didn't have a hit with it himself.[25] A half-hearted attempt was made to get it banned by the BBC for an imagined drug reference, when some genius posited the idea that sharing an 'umbrella' was code for illicit practices. (Was any word not suspected of being a drug reference in 1966?) Of course the song is a perfectly innocent vignette of a shy couple's tentative steps toward romance on their way home from work. Like its predecessor 'Look Through Any Window', the song makes no claims that the protagonists are in any way unique – it's their very ordinariness that makes the track itself so special.

The Hollies knew they had a hit on their hands and were determined to get it released before anyone else could. On the 18th May 1966, the day after a Manc gig-goer with a highly developed sense of perspective had called Bob Dylan 'Judas' for plugging his guitar in, The Hollies took just under

[25] He recorded it (and several other songs he'd watched become huge hits for others) for his 1968 album *The Graham Gouldman Thing*.

an hour to record 'Bus Stop' in Abbey Road Studio 3. The Beatles were next door mixing 'Got To Get You Into My Life', a supposed love song which really is all about drugs. No one attempted to ban that.

'Bus Stop' was released on both sides of the Atlantic less than a month after it was recorded. Any bittersweet feelings Graham Gouldman may have had about giving his song away were instantly forgotten when he heard The Hollies' recording. Once again the personal resonance of the song had inspired them to the very top of their game, and Gouldman was in raptures. To do his song justice required a band of top musicians that could handle three-part harmony as well as The Beatles, and who didn't write their own songs. The Hollies fitted the bill perfectly. If someone had suggested Gouldman replace Eric Haydock on bass, perhaps the course of musical history could have been changed. As it was, he had a few more years as a freelance songwriter ahead of him. As for The Hollies, recording Gouldman's Mancunian masterpiece did no less than unlock their collective muse. Their next album *For Certain Because* was entirely written by band members and thereafter the group released only self-penned singles, including the brilliant 'Carrie Anne', until Graham Nash's departure in 1968.

The USA, still in the thrall of all things British, was as delighted with The Hollies' 'Bus Stop' as Graham had been. The song's delicate North of England charm thrilled America's Anglophile record buyers nearly as much as the significantly less subtle 'Mrs Brown You've Got A Lovely Daughter' had done a year earlier. It peaked at No. 5 in mid-September and was the biggest US hit the band had in the sixties.[26] It also

[26] It was also their second biggest hit ever. 'Long Cool Woman In A Black Dress' reached No. 2 in 1972.

54

reached No. 5 in the UK, hit No. 1 in Canada and Sweden and made the Top 10 in Australia, Germany, Netherlands, New Zealand and Norway. In fact, it was so successful Mickie Most finally relented and allowed Herman's Hermits to record one of Graham's songs as a single.

It was the success that did it. Mickie Most had little interest in quality songwriting, he just needed Herman's Hermits' US releases to fit their image of daft-but-loveable Northern Englishmen. He was even prepared to capitalise on the success of the George Formbyesque 'Mrs Brown' by releasing Formby's signature tune 'Leaning On A Lamp Post' as a single, which the group had reluctantly recorded for their second movie, *Hold On!*.

He didn't care that the band hated it, of course, any more than he cared that they detested every single aspect of filming *Hold On!*. For him that was missing the point.[27] 'Leaning On A Lamp Post' reached No. 9 in the US in May, where it sat quite unabashed alongside such cerebral fare as Bob Dylan's 'Rainy Day Women #12 & 35' and 'Monday Monday' by the Mamas and Papas. That was the point.

While there's no arguing with Most's results (they had enough material to fill Volume 2 of their US greatest hits by November 1966), it did mean that the band would be forever preserved in American memory as a novelty act. It also meant that although Graham Gouldman was about to provide two of his finest songs for Herman's Hermits' next two singles, there was only room in their crowded US release schedule for one of them.

[27] The band had good reason to hate *Hold On!* as the plot makes *When The Boys Meet The Girls* look like *Citizen Kane*. When NASA decide to name a space capsule after the band, the US State Department attempts to discredit them so that the world won't think the USA is still a colony of Britain. It could be a documentary, couldn't it? The film was originally slated to be called *A Must To Avoid*, after the Hermits' next single, until someone realised that title was a film reviewer's dream.

The tacit agreement between the band, their manager and their producer to issue whatever they thought would appeal to their US fan base, no matter how facile, luckily didn't apply to the UK. As a result, even Mickie Most was willing to show a little more restraint when choosing what to release as a single at home.

Even though its thoughtful intelligence was at odds with the Hermits' American image, it's still astonishing that 'No Milk Today' wasn't released as a single in the States. The vocals from Noone, Hopwood and Green are outstanding, as is the production, particularly John Paul Jones's delicate string arrangement.[28] This was the first time a Hermits song had featured strings and it proved so successful that Most began to question whether a beat group was the most appropriate backing for Noone going forward. Especially given that, unlike the rest of the band, Peter Noone had moved to London by now and was available to record at a minute's notice. This gave rise to recurring rumours that the band didn't play on their records at all – an inaccurate assumption that Noone has made little effort to dispel over the years. The surviving members insist the practice was relatively rare, maintaining that nobody would have even commented had two of the session musicians Mickie Most utilised – Jimmy Page and John Paul Jones – not gone on to form the biggest band in the world.

The lyrical inspiration for 'No Milk Today' came from Graham Gouldman's father. He urged Graham to imagine the sadness behind something as simple as a note in a milk bottle. Graham responded to the challenge with a euphonious piece of Manc melancholia that inspired Peter Noone's finest vocal

---

[28] He also provided a far more florid string arrangement for Gouldman's own version of the song a year later.

performance. As well as the almost cinematic 'the bottle stands forlorn, a symbol of the dawn', there's a lovely pun on 'two/too up two/too down' as an illustration of both where the couple lived and the narrator's manic-depressive disposition. The upbeat tempo masking the minor chord progression is also a fitting metaphor for the tragedy that lurks beneath a seemingly affable life. Noone himself was in no doubt as to the song's merits: 'Personally, I think "No Milk Today" is Herman's Hermits' best recording, and perfectly captures the moment and the feel of Manchester terraced houses and what was the end of a British era.'

Most, believing a poignant evocation of Broughton's back-to-back houses wouldn't necessarily play in Bear Creek Alabama, made the American audience wait a year to hear it when it was issued as the B-side of 'A Kind of Hush'. He was probably mistaken because the song received significant US airplay and sufficient record buyers asked for it by name that it reached No. 35 in its own right. In the meantime the Hermits' American fans were treated to the Hermits' recording of Ray Davies's 'Dandy', a track on the Kinks' *Face To Face* album.[29] Its seaside postcard music and lyric, once again reminiscent of George Formby, were a perfect fit for the band, and its blend of silliness and knowing winks made it an ideal US single, but it wasn't a patch on 'No Milk Today'.

Perhaps realising it had been a mistake not releasing 'No Milk Today' in America, Most allowed fans on both sides of the Atlantic to hear Graham Gouldman's next Hermits single simultaneously. Despite 'East West' being even more melancholic than its predecessor, though no less convincing,

[29] The Kinks had been banned from touring the US in 1965, prompting a change in emphasis in Davies's songwriting to more English concerns. The American concert-goers loss was definitely pop music's gain.

its weary waltz perfectly captures the aching loneliness of the lyric. Again the orchestration is spot-on, particularly the chimes evoking the 'bells of home'. Though its themes are universal, for Gouldman, this 'homesick lament of a globetrotting popstar' is sung by someone missing a very specific place: 'It was always a very Mancunian song; it was about being away from Manchester, not being away from London or Amsterdam or Rome.'[30]

When the disillusioned troubadour, his thoughts filled with home, laments 'What a great life it must seem' the song radiates regret. It was, much to its author's delight, later covered by another product of Park Hospital, Davyhulme: self-confessed Hermits devotee Stephen Patrick Morrissey. Though Peter Noone made a fine job of the vocal, the sad lament was probably better suited to Morrissey's personality. Morrissey nails the wistful lyric so well it's difficult to listen to the Hermits' version without hearing his plaintive baritone. Whichever version you prefer, it's impossible to deny the song's power.

Taken as a whole, 'Look Through Any Window', 'Bus Stop', 'No Milk Today' and 'East West' form a unique and distinctly Mancunian quadrilogy. If they'd been released consecutively by a single artist, who's to say that history wouldn't hold them in as high regard as the other singles coming from the North West of England in 1965-66?

There is one more addition to Graham Gouldman's Mancunian oeuvre which was never released as a single, more's the pity. It was written for the Hermits' final cinematic venture, *Mrs Brown You've Got A Lovely Daughter*, the story

[30] The lyric is similar in subject matter to Paul Simon's 'Homeward Bound', though transatlantically transposed.

of a young Manchester band's adventures in London. With their greyhound. Clearly the filmmakers had learned several lessons from *Hold On!*. As it was filmed and set in England, the band's dialogue was much more authentic, and there were absolutely no spaceships. The plot even made sense, up to a point. Graham contributed the song 'It's Nice To Be Out In The Morning', which takes a trip round Manchester's more unusually-named boroughs and manages to be both misty-eyed and pragmatic at the same time. It's surely the only time either Besses o' th' Barn or Boggart Hole Clough will ever appear on a lyric sheet. It unequivocally nails its author's colours to the mast by including a whole verse dedicated to 'champions' Manchester United while champions-elect City don't get a mention. It also features the brilliantly evocative and largely horticulturally-accurate line, 'Ardwick Green where the grass is grey.' Quite what MGM's Hollywood executives made of it is anyone's guess.

Chapter 3
It's Getting Harder All The Time

The Mindbenders
A Groovy Kind Of Love

Wayne Fontana and the Mindbenders' time in the sun turned out to be shorter than the average Mancunian summer. On the back of 'The Game Of Love's success, they played several US dates with their Kennedy Street colleagues Herman's Hermits, which gave managers Harvey Lisberg and Ric Dixon plenty of time to compare notes on the intricacies of band management on the road. It also gave Eric Stewart his first encounter with the hysterical hordes of fans that had become the norm for the Hermits, and he was less than impressed. He considered himself a serious musician, and as the sound of twenty thousand teenagers screaming was more than enough to defeat the woefully inadequate PA systems provided, he found the whole process fairly pointless and not a little frightening. Wayne Fontana had problems of his own.

Like Herman's Hermits, The Mindbenders were forced to follow a punitive schedule. As well as the constant touring, for Mancs every other aspect of being in a band, apart from appearing on *Top of the Pops*, meant being away from home as well. Though both Harvey Lisberg and Ric Dixon were based at Kennedy Street in Manchester, the record industry itself was completely run from London. Any recording or interaction with their record company had to take place there; it simply wasn't possible for a Mancunian to put music to tape and sleep in his own bed. Most Northern musicians took the easy way out and moved down south, but The Mindbenders and the Hermits, to their credit, refused to follow suit. This inevitably took its toll on them both physically and mentally; Wayne in particular struggled with nervous exhaustion. In his case it was fuelled by the not necessarily unfounded fear that the band weren't 100% behind him. It didn't help that when his health forced him to miss a couple of shows, Eric Stewart was more than able to step in on vocals, dodgy sound or not – a fact that didn't go unnoticed by management.

Despite these issues, the US tour was enough of a success, at least in financial terms, for Dixon to swiftly arrange another. But it was clear that things were not quite as they should be in The Mindbenders camp. For a start, the next two singles Clint Ballard Jr. gave them singularly failed to replicate the success of 'The Game Of Love'. This was a shame in the case of 'It's Just A Little Bit Too Late' as it was a fantastic record which had everything its predecessor had – a brilliant vocal, a nod to Bo Diddley, a great guitar solo and Eric Stewart's memorable backing vocal sighs that would later become a Buzzcocks trademark – while being nothing like it.

'She Needs Love', on the other hand, deserved everything it didn't get, despite Ric Rothwell playing out of his skin. (Apparently great drums aren't sufficient to make a record a hit – who knew?) Put simply, the record wasn't anywhere near good enough and even Jack Baverstock seemed off his game. If he'd been paying attention he'd never have mixed the vocals so high on a song with such a lousy lyric.

'It's Just A Little Bit Too Late' made No. 20 in the UK and No. 45 in the US, while 'She Needs Love' struggled to No. 32 in Britain and did nothing at all in America. Perhaps seeing the writing on the wall, while recording their second album Eric Stewart badgered Baverstock for some insights into the arcane art of production, which was beginning to interest him more than badly-amplified live performance. It wasn't immediately forthcoming. For their early records

Baverstock, like many a London producer, wouldn't even let the band into the control room till he'd finished. The idea that the band were the most important element in the making of a hit record and that their opinions were more significant or even equal to those of the producer, the manager or the record company, was a long way from universal acceptance in 1965. In fact it was mainly confined to Abbey Road Studio 2. It only became the norm as the sixties turned into the seventies, and as such it never had much impact on the Mindbenders' or Herman's Hermits' careers at all.[31] Eric Stewart persisted, however, and was eventually allowed to shadow Baverstock and pick up some of the engineering skills that would prove crucial for the next part of his career.

Wayne Fontana and the Mindbenders' second album, the snappily titled *Eric, Rick, Wayne And Bob – It's Wayne Fontana And The Mindbenders*,[32] faired as badly as 'She Needs Love'. It was in much the same vein as their first album, and featured more of those R&B numbers every band in the North West had in their set. Again they only managed a couple of originals, both of which had been previously released as the flip side of singles. When it came to songwriting, the band's only real motivation was 50% of the single royalties. Wayne was becoming increasingly preoccupied, and vocals were shared with Eric Stewart and Ric Rothwell. Of course, as musicians, the Mindbenders were never less than brilliant throughout the album. If Wayne Fontana had been more on point, who knows what they could have achieved?

But that was pretty much it. Wayne grew more disillusioned with the band and the Mindbenders were in no mood to sit down and work on the causes of his unhappiness. Ric

---

[31] Martin Hannett never much cared for the idea either.

[32] (Sic). As well as being a terrible title, they added an extraneous 'k' to Ric's name.

Rothwell told the erstwhile Glyn Ellis he was welcome to 'take your ego trip and piss off' whenever he wanted, and one night he did precisely that, midway through a gig. 'It's all yours,' Fontana told Eric Stewart, and exited stage left. The gig continued uninterrupted.

The band were understandably furious. One of their main motivators for carrying on was to show Fontana they didn't need him. According to Eric Stewart, who was still seething years later, 'All we lost was our tambourine player.'

Perhaps surprisingly, Fontana (the label) were happy to offer both sides of the split a record deal, but management was a different story. Wayne was not of a mind to share his manager with people he believed had been undermining him for months. He made his position clear to Ric Dixon in no uncertain terms, telling him, 'You either manage them, or you manage me.' But he didn't get the response he'd expected. Dixon, sensing that Eric Stewart was a better prospect long term than Wayne, retorted, 'Sorry Wayne, I'll manage them.' And that was that.

The winners in this less-than-ideal situation were Fontana Records, at least at first. Under new management, and after a couple of fairly respectable UK hits, Wayne hit the big time again courtesy of Graham Gouldman, who though he had an office in Kennedy Street and was functioning as the de facto in-house writer, had no problem giving a song to the recently-departed Mr Fontana. He was happy to place songs wherever he could. The song he gave him, 'Pamela, Pamela', was a saccharine piece of whimsy,[33] but perfect for Wayne,

[33] 'The Wombling Song' borrows its phrasing wholesale. Eric Stewart later asserted that 'Pamela, Pamela' was actually written by Godley & Creme as part of an aborted musical that was sold to Kennedy Street and Gouldman when they were short of funds. Gouldman however has called the song one of his favourite compositions and let's face it, he doesn't really need to claim songs he didn't write.

both song and artist possessing an underlying intelligence that's not always apparent. The song piles on more and more stock nostalgic images until it verges on parody, then has 'the harshness of life' pull the rug on it all at the end. It got to No. 11 in the UK and was the biggest – and last – hit Wayne Fontana ever had. However, he remains a charismatic live performer to this day, illness and the odd spell in prison permitting.

Eric Stewart was a gifted guitarist with no ambition to be a frontman, but was thrust into the spotlight when his singer departed. They couldn't be sure that their audience would stick by them so for the Wayne Fontana-less Mindbenders their next choice of single was crucial. All it would take is another 'Stop, Look And Listen' or 'She Needs Love' and Eric Stewart could well have found himself back on National Road trading in his guitar for a new air rifle. Luckily for them, they were gifted 'A Groovy Kind Of Love',[34] a song that would give them as much success as they'd enjoyed with Wayne.

In 1965, Toni Wine was a 17-year-old music student who was financing her way through college by working as an in-house songwriter at Screen Gems in New York. She had the idea of basing a pop song around the Rondo movement of Muzio Clementi's 'Sonatina in G Major', as you do. She was probably inspired by the success of The Toys' recent single 'A Lover's Concerto', which similarly pilfered a G major classical melody, in this case Christian Petzold's 'Minuet in G Major'.[35] She asked fellow Screen Gems employee Carol

[34] In the interest of full disclosure, this song was the first dance at my wedding. I'll try to be unbiased.

[35] The piece was incorrectly credited to J.S. Bach at the time, Petzold was only identified as the composer in 1977.

Bayer to provide a lyric and the two discussed basing it around the word 'groovy' which, although it was a jazz term that had been around since the twenties, was very much the mot du jour in 1965. Interviewed in 2007, Wine stated they got the idea from Simon & Garfunkel's '59th Street Bridge Song', but given that 'Groovy Kind Of Love' was released before it, that seems unlikely. They first offered the song to Lesley Gore of 'It's My Party' fame, but her producer Shelby Singleton wouldn't countenance a song with a slang word in the title, so it ended up being recorded by US vocal duo Diane and Annita. Previously singers with Ray Anthony's Big Band, they hit on the song as a way of changing their image to something more hip and happening. Their distinctly daffy version, featuring some chintzy strings and an ill-advised and decidedly creepy baby-talk vocal,[36] only saw the light of day in France as part of an EP where it wasn't even the featured number. That was 'One By One', as previously recorded by The Mockingbirds, which wasn't brilliant but at least the vocals weren't disturbing.

That would have been it for 'A Groovy Kind Of Love' but Screen Gems' London manager Jack McGraw stumbled across it and decided it would be perfect for The Mindbenders. Quite how he came to this conclusion is a mystery – it's hard to imagine that anyone hearing Diane and Annita's version would think of pitching it to a well-drilled R&B beat group, but it turned out to be a perfect fit.

Bayer Sager (she married record producer Andrew Sager in 1970) later recalled that 'A Groovy Kind Of Love' was completed in twenty minutes. The song contains some

[36] Comparing the vocal to that of Carol Bayer Sager's massively annoying 'You're Moving Out Today' would seem to suggest that she sang lead on the Diane and Annita record.

terrible rhymes, and at first glance it's not exactly cerebral. However, the classical melody is so strong it imbues the lyric with enough emotional weight to transcend its gimmicky genesis, at least when it's not sung by someone trying to sound five years old. It's a mark of its veiled ingenuity that the song manages to be timeless even while availing itself of such sixties-centric terminology as 'groovy' and 'turn me on'. Moreover, The Mindbenders' simple arrangement makes a real virtue of their sparse line-up – there are some strings and female backing vocals but these are tastefully discreet. The record is a virtual blueprint for the lovelorn power-pop Pete Shelley's Buzzcocks would unleash a decade later, albeit significantly speeded up. Despite its brevity, the public on both sides of the Atlantic certainly took 'A Groovy Kind Of Love' to heart. It reached No. 2 in the UK in January 1966 and reached the same number in the US in May when it was belatedly released from The Mindbenders album named after it.

Not surprisingly, The Mindbenders stuck with Wine & Bayer for their next two singles – the remarkably soulful '(Can't Live With You) Can't Live Without You'[37] and the awkward and strangely dissatisfying 'Ashes To Ashes'. Of the two, 'Ashes To Ashes' did slightly better chart-wise, getting them to No. 14 in the UK and 44 in the US.

The band's big problem was the disconnect between the material they played brilliantly live – R&B in the style of the early Stones or The Pretty Things – and the songs they were given in order to secure a hit. As they were reliant on others to provide material they remained artistically frustrated. The answer should have been obvious, but strangely the band

[37] Sometimes billed as 'Can't Live With You (Can't Live Without You)'. They were parenthetically challenging times.

and their management remained as blind to the possibility of releasing a self-penned single as they had been when Wayne was on board. This was despite the fact that Eric Stewart's 'You Don't Know About Love', the B-side of 'Ashes To Ashes', was at least as good a song and vastly more suited to the band, though the lyrics were a bit soppy.

To be fair, there still weren't many band originals to choose from. Their first Wayne-less album, called *The Mindbenders* in the UK and *A Groovy Kind Of Love* in the US, only featured the standard two, one for the B-side of each single. Their next single, released at the end of 1966, was written by The Zombies' Rod Argent. 'I Want Her, She Wants Me'[38] was a very contemporary-sounding but largely hook-free number, built round the kind of crotchet piano stabs that everyone was using at that time.[39] It had as little chart success as its follow-up, 'We'll Talk About It Tomorrow', which came courtesy of their old friends Wine & Bayer.

Publishers Screen Gems who, as the name implies, were primarily movie producers, sought to bolster The Mindbenders' waning chart profile by including both sides of their next single in their upcoming vignette of London life *To Sir, With Love*, which meant that the band's name had a prominent presence in the credits. This was a proper film, not like the hastily-produced fare the Hermits were forced to endure. It was a socially aware kitchen-sink drama, written and directed by no less than James Clavell,[40] which enjoyed considerable critical acclaim and significant box office returns.

Unfortunately, not even the sight of the band soundtracking

---

[38] It later appeared on The Zombies' critically acclaimed but waywardly spelled *Odessey & Oracle*.

[39] E.g. The Kinks' 'Dead End Street', 'Daydream' by the Lovin' Spoonful, 'Penny Lane'.

[40] Co-writer of *The Great Escape*, *633 Squadron* and author of *Shogun*.

Sidney Poitier's groovy dance moves and Judy Geeson's white crochet dress was enough to score them a significant hit. The A-side, 'It's Getting Harder All The Time', was brilliant as well, a real mod classic with punchy guitar, especially the solo, and driving percussion (seems they didn't miss Wayne's tambourine playing after all). It was finally a satisfactory compromise between the band's favoured idiom and proper pop catchiness, which makes its failure something of a mystery. It was a bit let down by the lyric, another ho-hum unrequited love song.[41] But since poor lyrics rarely affect a song's success, its failure can only have been due to the fact that The Mindbenders' ship had finally sailed.

Ironically, the film's title song did give The Mindbenders their final brush with success, as they provided muted and largely uncredited backing for Lulu. The single 'To Sir, With Love' was a massive hit in Britain and America at the tail end of 1967. By the time it was released, The Mindbenders' classic line-up was no more; Ric Rothwell departed the drum stool soon after they finished their second album. That album, *With Woman In Mind*, included a song by their friend and office colleague Graham Gouldman: 'Schoolgirl', a sensationalist tale of underage pregnancy.

The band soldiered on with a new drummer, Paul Hancox, and tried everything they could to secure another hit. When Harvey Lisberg secured the publishing rights to The Box Tops' 'The Letter' on a trip to New York, they hastily recorded a version with Graham Gouldman producing, in the hope of beating the original to a UK hit. It didn't work. The Mindbenders' version[42] reached No. 42 in September

[41] How come no one ever wrote songs about not being in love eh, Eric?

[42] The B-side 'My New Day And Age', written by Eric Stewart, saw him despairing at the rise of the tower blocks that were filling the Manchester skyline.

1967 and The Box Tops reached No. 5 the same month. In desperation they re-recorded 'Schoolgirl' and attempted to make it sound as 1967 as possible. The song didn't really suit the psychedelic rock treatment and not even a headline-generating BBC ban could drum up enough interest to make it a hit. After one more single, Bob Lang jumped ship and Stewart asked Graham Gouldman to take over on bass. With that, one of the seventies most successful partnerships was finally in place, but unfortunately it was all too late for The Mindbenders. Gouldman penned their final single, the risible 'Uncle Joe, The Ice Cream Man', which really is as bad as it sounds. While the band were recording it at Olympic in Barnes they had a visit from Mick Jagger, who was working next door. 'Why are you singing this shit?' he enquired, not unreasonably. Neither Stewart nor Gouldman had an answer.

Chapter 4
Big Boys Don't Cry

The Birth Of Strawberry Studios

It was obvious that The Mindbenders career as a recording act was over. Since 'A Groovy Kind Of Love' had provided them with a US No. 2, the following three years had seen them drift further down the Hot 100, to the point where 'Uncle Joe, The Ice Cream Man' couldn't even give them a 99. Graham was first to jump ship: he had his primary career as a songwriter to return to, so the demise of The Mindbenders wasn't such a big deal for him.

Eric had secured a couple of lucrative B-sides during his time with The Mindbenders so he wasn't facing penury, but he certainly wasn't as financially secure as Graham. In any case he wasn't the type to stop working. With a new house and family to support, he was forced to take a version of the band around the cabaret and working men's clubs of the North just to earn a living. Of course, lots of bands found themselves in a similar position as the sixties wore on, and many took to it like ducks to water. Peter Noone had always aspired to be an all-round entertainer, Freddie Garrity's act was tailor-made for cabaret, and Wayne Fontana soon developed a self-deprecating shtick that went down a bomb on the chicken-in-a-basket circuit. Eric wasn't cut out for it at all. To him, The Mindbenders were the original power trio – a hard rocking proto-Cream that could play authentic R&B with the best of them. Instead they were forced to churn out limpid ballads to disinterested punters whose primary concern was when the bingo would start. It was more than a little disheartening. Things came to a head at a gig in Wales when the band was ordered to stop playing because they were affecting bar sales. Eric, who was already smarting from the fact that the promoter hadn't even bothered to name them on the posters,[43] called it a day.

Still, Eric wasn't the type to wallow in self-pity. For some time he'd been recording his demos in a room above the Nield & Hardy music shop on Great Underbank in Stockport – the grandly named 'Inter-City Studios'. In reality it was an empty room with a tape recorder and a couple of microphones, but Eric believed it had potential. It was run by Peter Tattersall, a former roadie for Billy J Kramer & the Dakotas, who used what money he had spare from his day job in a bakery to kit out his glorified rehearsal room. The sound-proofing consisted of egg boxes sellotaped to the walls and no recording could be done while the shop was open. Basic as it was, it was about as good as it got north of Watford in those days, and several bands, including the Hermits and The Mindbenders, had recorded demos there, though nothing had ever been commercially released. When the management of Neild & Hardy decided that a staff canteen would be a better use of their 3rd floor than a scruffy demo studio, Tattersall knew he'd never be able to pull off a move to new premises on his own. He approached Eric, who he knew was keen to make a move into engineering and production. As it turned out, Eric wasn't interested in running an attic demo studio, he'd had a much loftier ambition for some time. If, he reasoned, Danny Betesh, Harvey Lisberg, Ric Dixon and the rest of Kennedy Street could run a highly successful music management business without moving to London, against the prevailing wisdom, then why should every other aspect of the industry have to be based there?

[43] 'Top Welsh Tenor plus support group'. Who got the bigger dressing room is lost to history.

During the last days of The Mindbenders, mindful that he had never really finished his education, Eric had completed a course in interior design at the London College of Domestic Arts – a correspondence course, naturally. He was moving nowhere. He'd already designed some of the rooms in Harvey's new house and he believed that, given the right premises, he could create a recording studio at least the equal of the ones he'd been forced to schlep down south to for the previous five years.

Eric and Peter began searching the local area and soon found the perfect place at No. 3, Waterloo Road, Stockport. Unfortunately, one of the reasons it was perfect for Eric's vision was that it was completely empty, a blank canvas. Though neither of them were afraid of hard work, Eric soon realised that the £800 he'd earmarked from his savings wouldn't be nearly enough to source everything. He buttonholed his friend and erstwhile musical partner Graham Gouldman, who, excited by Eric's singular vision, and against the advice of everyone he asked, agreed to inject the not-inconsiderable sum of £2,000[44] to become a financial partner in this new enterprise. They set to work, with Eric and Tattersall performing most of the tasks, both conceptual and manual. Eric insulated walls, painted ceilings and spent many hours mixing cement before he ever mixed a track.

When it became clear that further finance was required they approached the local banks. The problem they faced was that the bank managers and finance gurus of Manchester had no idea what was involved in building a recording studio. How could they? No one had ever done it before – the long-haired bohemians sitting in their office might as well have been asking for money to build a spaceship. What was needed was someone

[44] About £33,000 as of 2017.

to grant the enterprise an air of credibility, so Eric turned to his old manager, Ric Dixon. In the interests of rationalisation, The Mindbenders had left him and been managing themselves for a time, but Ric was big enough not to bear a grudge and agreed to place the name and weight of Kennedy Street behind the fledgling venture. With this it was possible to secure the finance they needed to complete the project.

It's worth emphasising this again, when Eric Stewart first pondered the possibility of building a professional-standard recording studio outside London, he was completely alone. The thought hadn't struck anyone else at all. It certainly didn't occur to The Beatles, who at around the same time found themselves with colossal amounts of cash to spend and the very real possibility that the tax man would have it if they didn't. Imagine the publicity, investment and urban renewal they could have brought to Liverpool (and God knows Liverpool needed investment in 1968) if they'd located Apple Corps on Matthew Street. At that time the only significant development in prospect for Liverpool's most famous street was British Rail's plan to turn The Cavern into a ventilation shaft. The idea of giving something back to the city that birthed them wasn't even considered. Instead, The Beatles, four working-class lads who had spent their youth hanging round Penny Lane's tram sheds and beneath the Docker's Umbrella, installed their sumptuously liveried head office and shop on Savile Row.[45] In Mayfair, of all places, the richest area in the richest city in the country.

[45] They had plans for a studio too, but none of the band had anything approaching Eric's determination or knowledge. They handed the task to John's drug mule 'Magic' Alex Mardas, who instead of the promised 72-track studio delivered nothing more than some holes in the cellar walls and a homemade mixing desk that didn't work. Ah, the sixties! As recording for *Let It Be* was due to start they had to call EMI's engineers in to quickly get a basic studio up and running. By the time a proper studio had been established, The Beatles were no more.

It was obvious to all concerned that the new venture in Stockport was not a continuation of Inter-City, and a new name for the studio was required. Eric decided to call it 'Strawberry Studios' after his favourite Beatles song. On one level, the name was entirely apt, as at that time 'Strawberry Fields Forever' was probably the greatest piece of studio recording and innovation ever committed to tape.[46] It was also one of the first examples of a record where the production is more important than the song itself.[47] On another level the name was palpably ironic, as it served to highlight the fact that the only thing The Beatles ever gave to Liverpool was to locate a couple of songs there. Strawberry Studios, on the other hand, was a gift to Manchester that would foster, shape and in some ways define its creative output for the next 30 years. 'You could tell it was built with love rather than profit in mind,' was how the studio's first female engineer, Julia Adamson, later described Strawberry's unique atmosphere.

*

Graham Gouldman's need to keep working following his departure from The Mindbenders prompted him to take a job as a songwriter for hire in New York. In 1968, Harvey Lisberg, who as ever knew the next big thing when he saw it, introduced him to Jerry Kasenetz and Jeff Katz, two astute, if ruthless, music producers. They'd realised that the current vogue to be seen as 'album artists' by The Beatles, The Stones *et al* had left an exploitable and lucrative gap in the singles chart. With unusual self-awareness they called the musical genre they created to fill this gap 'bubblegum',

[46] It can be argued it still is.

[47] 'Tomorrow Never Knows' being another.

which they picked to reflect the fact that the records would appeal to kids and were essentially weightless. So they could maximise their output they didn't stick to one artist, they issued singles by several all-but fictitious bands such as the 1910 Fruitgum Company[48] and Ohio Express.[49] They'd originally approached Lisberg when they realised he was from Manchester hoping he could hook them up with Freddie Garrity, as they thought the Dreamers would be a good addition to their bubblegum roster. However, as the sheer rapaciousness of this business model meant they were constantly on the look-out for new material, Lisberg suggested they speak to Gouldman. They must have been thrilled, if not a little puzzled, when a songwriter of Graham's calibre signed on as a song hack.

Quite what he was thinking, at least initially, is less clear, but he gave it his best shot. He spent a year in New York, on and off. He lived from a hotel room and commuted to an airless office every day to churn out the requisite amount of fluff from ten till six. In truth it made him ill, but he'd signed on the dotted line and didn't want to let anyone down. Fortunately for everyone, the birth of Strawberry Studios came at the perfect time. 'I've got involved in this studio back in Manchester. I want to take all the stuff we're recording here, and do it with my own guys back in England,' he announced. He saw an opportunity to get out of the dreadful position he was in and at the same time secure a block-booking for the fledging studio that would give them financial security for months.

---

[48] 'Simon Says', based on the children's game, and 'Goody Goody Gumdrops', amongst others. Cerebral stuff.

[49] 'Yummy Yummy Yummy (I've Got Love In My Tummy)'. Massively annoying, but I bet you're singing it at this very moment.

Kasenetz and Katz, despite some initial reluctance, agreed, with the proviso that their producer Ritchie Cordell come along to supervise production. This was perfect for all concerned; it gave Eric further exposure to professional production techniques and enabled Graham to bring another couple of friends on board to bolster the songwriting and recording team (and stop him going crackers producing drivel on his own).

Lol Creme, who'd written the B-side of Graham's first single, and Kevin Godley, The Mockingbirds' drummer, had been working together for some time.[50] They'd both recently qualified as graphic designers and were doing all they could to avoid conventional employment. They'd seen their fellow students' artistic ambitions crushed by the cold office environments of advertising agencies and were determined it wouldn't happen to them. Luckily, the ever-astute Lisberg and Dixon could see their artistic potential even if no one else could. Even they weren't sure in which branch of the arts that potential would blossom, however, so they placed the duo on a retainer of a fiver a week each. They set them to work as glorified odd-job men, drawing posters, designing book displays and even painting a mural in Lisberg's home. They also encouraged their songwriting. Lisberg introduced them to the Yardbirds' old manager Giorgio Gomelsky, who was sufficiently impressed with their songs to offer them a one album deal. Gomelsky gave them the ludicrous name Frabjoy and Runcible Spoon[51]

[50] As well as Godley and Creme, Manchester music legend Peter Cowap was also drafted in to help on some of the recording. Cowap had been a member of The Country Gents, The Manchester Mob, High Society (with Gouldman), The Measles and The Bujjies, amongst others.

[51] After Edward Lear. Ah, the sixties! (2)

and summoned them to London to begin recording. The album was never completed (Gomelsky was nowhere near as financially efficient as Lisberg or Dixon) and only one single, 'I'm Beside Myself'/'Animal Song'[52] ever saw the light of day. Unlike the rest of the Frabjoy material, both tracks were recorded at Strawberry, with Eric on guitar and Graham on bass. Though the single inevitably sank without trace, they all enjoyed the session and the four of them set to work producing copious amounts of bubblegum for Kasenetz-Katz. They kept their session money, but all of the studio fees were ploughed straight back into Strawberry.

As it turned out, Kasenetz and Katz did sign up Freddie and the Dreamers. One of the biggest successes to emerge from the Strawberry bubblegum sessions was 'Susan's Tuba', which though billed as a Dreamers single was actually down to Gouldman, Stewart, Creme and Godley. It was clearly modelled on 'Good Morning Starshine' from the musical *Hair*,[53] a song so preposterous that Freddie had taken to performing it in his cabaret act. The lyric of 'Susan's Tuba' sounds like the result of a band competition to see who could come up with the worst version of 'Good Morning Starshine's ridiculous 'Tooby ooby walla, nooby abba naba' line. If it was, then Graham won hands down, and his resultant gift to the world of song was 'Ooby dooby dooba, Susan's on the tuba'. To his everlasting astonishment, Graham's deliberate attempt to write as poor a song as possible sold a million copies, mainly in non-English speaking European countries,

[52] 'I'm Beside Myself' is a competent (if forgettable) piece of folk-rock; 'Animal Song' is much better, almost a Manc Simon & Garfunkel, (which is precisely how Gomelsky planned to market them) but the lyric is terrible. As an advert for the new studio, however, both sides are perfect: they sound great.

[53] *Hair* also contained a song called 'Manchester, England' coincidentally enough. It's lousy.

unsurprisingly.[54] The chances of it appearing on his CV any time soon are pretty low, however.

The fact that the bubblegum remit was so narrow during this period meant that Strawberry's in-house musicians had to look elsewhere for creative fulfilment. The music they produced, though basic in concept, often boasted ingenious production and inspired instrumentation. In fact, the songs they worked on could not have been better vehicles for increasing their knowledge of studio technique.[55] Removed from the pursuit of artistic excellence, and in order to preserve their sanity, all four of them actively sought to expand what it was possible to achieve in a recording studio. They accomplished this both by using what equipment they had in new and innovative ways, and crucially for Strawberry Studios' future, by adding to that equipment whenever they had spare cash. Eric in particular threw himself completely into the task at hand, often acting as engineer, producer, singer and musician during the course of a single session. He also took pains to engineer and produce studio bookings by other artists, no matter how they differed from his own musical tastes.[56] Eventually there was no one in the country with a better understanding of where the art of recording was going.

[54] In the late sixties there was something of a vogue for these nonsense lyrics, kicked off, as ever, by The Beatles: 'goo goo g'joob' from 'I Am The Walrus'. Top of the heap was 'Zabadak' by Dave Dee, Dozy, Beaky Mick & Tich, the chorus of which contains not a single real word.

[55] E.g. 'Sausalito' credited to Ohio Express (the lyric might have come from sticking a pin in a map, but the guitars sound massive); 'Umbopo', a plaintive ballad they recorded twice (you'd be surprised how much emotion a man can put into the phrase 'There ain't no Umbopo') and 'Roll On' by Doctor Father, which could pass for an outtake from *Exile On Main St.* but for the fact that the drum sound is too good.

[56] Or football loyalties. In the studio's early days he and Tattersall produced sessions by Manchester City ('The Boys In Blue'); Leeds United (the imaginatively titled 'Leeds United'); Everton ('For Ever Everton') and Bury FC ('Up The Shakers', which mainly featured fans and was credited to The Bury-Tones.) Classics all.

Though they were still a fairly provincial outfit, the arrival of the studios' new Apex 4-track machine and state-of-the-art control desk in 1970 (they'd previously had two 2-track machines slaved together) allowed them to expand their musical horizons hugely. The very first track recorded on the new machine became a massive hit all over Europe. It happened one evening as Stewart, Godley and Creme[57] were testing the new tape's bouncing[58] capabilities by endlessly tracking an undemanding drum beat. To keep interest up after Godley had spent hours playing the monotonous pattern, Creme began singing a simple repeated phrase over the top of it. When the bass drum mic picked up the plaintive vocal the trio liked the result so much they added some more instrumentation (but not a lot) to complete the track. In the process they tried every studio technique they could think of, including accidentally wiping some of the tracks, until a song that was barely more than a nursery rhyme was complete. The crunching drum sound they'd managed to capture was a particular revelation, at least the equal of the Plastic Ono Band's recent 'Instant Karma', and the recording proved it was possible for English bands to reproduce the Phil Spector 'Wall of Sound' by travelling no further than Waterloo Road, SK1.

That said, the track would probably have been forgotten but for Dick Leahy, A&R manager of Philips Records. Leahy had been friends with Eric since the Mindbender days and was fascinated with the idea that a proper studio could exist

[57] Gouldman was in New York with Kasenetz-Katz.

[58] 'Bouncing' is a standard studio technique where multiple tracks are re-recorded onto a single one, thereby freeing up those tracks for more recording. Obviously this results in some loss of fidelity, but decent engineers can find interesting ways to disguise this, and 10cc eventually used the technique to produce a sonic masterpiece. As tape machines with more and more tracks became available, reliance on bouncing declined commensurately.

outside London. While in Manchester on business he decided to pay them a visit and happened to be in the studio as they were playing the track back. He could tell straightaway it was a hit; in fact he was so convinced he gave them a princely £500 on the spot to secure the rights.

Eric, who'd never even been offered any kind of advance before, was understandably thrilled. Such was his ambition for the studio he was in the process of downsizing his home to free up some more working capital. Fired by Leahy's enthusiasm, he took his house off the market and 'Neanderthal Man' by Hotlegs, the track written to test a piece of studio equipment (you'd be hard-pressed to even call it a song), sold two million copies worldwide. And more importantly, the song's huge sonic landscape was the major part of its appeal. The studio itself was the most important instrument on the record. Strawberry Studios had arrived.

Chapter 5
The Devil Will Find Work For Idle Hands To Do

The Humble Beginnings Of Pluto Studios

After 1968, the Hermits' hits were mainly confined to Europe. Though they'd previously been one of the biggest bands in the US, they were forced to watch several singles make the UK Top 10 while simultaneously failing to reach the Billboard Hot 100.[59] Their US label, MGM, had serious financial difficulties, despite being part of one of the biggest film companies in the world. When the Hermits' US fanbase began to shift their loyalties to The Monkees, who boasted their own loveable Manc ex-*Coronation Street*er in the shape of Davy Jones, MGM had neither the wherewithal nor the inclination to fund the necessary compensatory promotion. By 1969, Mickie Most had had enough of handing over proven hits[60] only to see them die a death in America, so MGM effectively stopped releasing Herman's Hermits records.

Peter Noone had always fancied himself as an all-round entertainer and was keen to expand his career into film and TV acting. So, with Herman pursuing external interests and the US demanding less and less of their attention, the Hermits found themselves with significant time on their hands. When not promoting records or playing live, Hopwood and Leckenby's main job was contributing to the Hermits' songwriting, though their output was mainly confined to

[59] E.g. 'Sunshine Girl' (July 1968: UK No. 8, US No. 101) and 'Something's Happening' (November 1968: UK No. 6, US No. 130)

[60] The marvellous 'My Sentimental Friend' being the biggest (UK No. 2), written by John Carter who wrote 'Can't You Hear My Heartbeat?' The song is notable for having far more emotional heft than Noone is normally given credit for.

album tracks and B-sides.[61] When they mentioned to their Kennedy Street colleague Eric Stewart that they were sick of traipsing to London to demo these tracks, he introduced them to Inter-City Studios. They booked in straight away, but they weren't massively impressed, realising that for a reasonable outlay they could probably create as good a set-up themselves. Without any real prior knowledge they bought a tape machine, set it up in Hopwood's house and began to fathom how it worked. When Noone announced he was taking three months off to star in a TV movie[62] they decided that would be enough time to do things properly and move to dedicated premises.

As fate would have it, a room on the top floor of 3 Waterloo Road, Stockport became available. While Eric Stewart and Peter Tattersall were busy transforming the ground floor, Hopwood, Lek and engineer Tony Cockle got busy installing a rudimentary 2-track facility in the small office above their heads. Unlike Strawberry, Pluto's owners didn't have plans initially to make their studio a going commercial concern. In truth they didn't have much of a plan at all, they were making it up as they went along, but the more strategic activity going on downstairs made them realise it might be an idea to offer something unique, or risk having the whole exercise turn into an expensive vanity project. In need of an ideas man, and because they also needed someone to run the place when the Hermits went back on the road, Hopwood contacted their old roadie Ric Turton, who he knew had been

[61] One of the best of which was 'Gaslight Street', a lovely Monkees-esque ballad on the *There's A Kind of Hush All Over the World* LP. The weirdest was a distinctly strange instrumental they provided for the soundtrack of the film *Mrs Brown, You've Got A Lovely Daughter*: 'Daisy Chain' (Part I)', a bizarre psychedelic oddball which wouldn't have sounded out of place in the Haçienda in 1990.

[62] *Pinocchio*, starring the 21-year-old Noone as the eponymous puppet (he really didn't give a shit, did he?) and Burl Ives as Geppetto. It aired on 8th December 1968 in the US and in the UK a year later.

involved in recording in America.[63] Ric suggested they look at recording jingles and soundtracks for advertisements, with an eye to getting an in at Granada TV.[64] Since the banning of 'Ad-Mags' (adverts disguised as dramas) in 1963, many of the advertisements on local TV stations such as Granada were little more than slideshows with a single voice-over, broadcast live. Turton had realised that newly available cartridge technology, widely used in the US but completely new in the UK, could transform the industry. The cartridges meant that pre-recorded musical accompaniment and sound effects could be added to voice-overs, along with a pulse to control the images. This made it possible for the sound on these local adverts to be as good as the high-budget filmed ones, even if the images weren't. This unique offering was the making of the studio. Commercial recording subsidised the band-recording side of Pluto's business for the whole of its existence.

The fact that Pluto was situated up a flight of stairs from Strawberry proved advantageous in a number of ways. As well as enabling them to pick up bookings from acts who couldn't

[63] Turton was a former DJ at the Plaza in Manchester who'd been so impressed when the Hermits played there in 1964 he signed on as their road manager. He'd subsequently worked as a DJ on Radio Caroline (as 'Ric Jonns') before emigrating to the States and becoming one of the first English DJs on commercial radio, which didn't exist in the UK at the time. The tragic death of his young wife in a road accident triggered a nervous breakdown and after a brief spell in a US mental institution he returned to Manchester to convalesce.

[64] Granada TV was always way ahead of the other regional TV networks in its forward-thinking attitude and has continually played a massive role in the pre-eminence of the Manchester and Liverpool music scenes. (They employed Tony Wilson, for a start.) Unlike the other regional network bosses, who saw local TV as a stepping stone to work in London, Granada founder Sidney Bernstein saw producing TV 'from the North' as a goal in itself. He refused to employ people who wouldn't move up from London, and when asked why he picked Manchester as the base for his TV empire he replied, 'I think that what Manchester sees today, London will see eventually.' Amen, brother.

quite afford the rates downstairs, Eric Stewart's insatiable appetite for new equipment meant that Pluto got first refusal on his cast-offs. This meant they could upgrade at regular intervals for a reduced outlay. When Granada included Pluto's sound recording technology on their advertising rate card, and the other regional stations quickly followed suit, Pluto swiftly became an economically viable going concern.

Once the Hermits began working again, it soon became clear that Keith Hopwood's interest in this new venture was not matched by Derek Leckenby's. Lek just wanted to play guitar. Though he continued to write and record songs with Hopwood, he gave up his interest in Pluto, perfectly amicably, and Keith brought in Malcolm Rowe to replace him.[65] Malcolm was a drummer by trade who Keith had played with pre-Hermits. He had little technical knowledge, but he was sufficiently enthusiastic to ensure he became an integral part of Pluto's set up, both as an engineer and later as Keith's co-composer.

The Hermits, meanwhile, were coming to an impasse. Rightly or wrongly, and with the tacit encouragement of Mickie Most, Peter Noone decided he didn't need to be part of a band. He'd even tried altering the billing to 'Peter Noone with Herman's Hermits', which didn't make any sense at all. Certainly he believed he'd be financially better off solo, even though he'd been on a higher percentage than the rest of the band all along. With no small degree of irony, one of the last singles they released as a band was 'Here Comes The Star',

[65] Ric Turton, who never sat still for long, had since departed on his never-ending search for his next gig. He subsequently enjoyed a short stint as Keith Chegwin's manager, became a publicity agent at Sunderland FC, worked as a bus driver and ended his days as a photographer on *The Beccles And Bungay Journal*, where he died at the far too young age of 42. What a life.

the lyric of which contains the lines 'Look at me now, I'm the loneliest guy in the world; People say he's a star and he's sure to go far, ain't he pretty; Now the stage is bare, knowing you're not there.' On 5th November 1971, his 24th birthday, Noone left the band.

The Hermits carried on and signed to RCA in the UK. They didn't have to look far to fill the respective gaps vacated by Noone, De Lane Lea Studios and Mickie Most. Strawberry's bubblegum collaborator, Peter Cowap, took over on vocals and initial recordings were done at Strawberry with Eric Stewart handling production duties. They released two promising singles, the country-tinged 'She's A Lady', and 'The Man',[66] which sounded like Nicks-Buckingham era Fleetwood Mac three years before Fleetwood Mac did. The band's whole sound was much more West Coast than West Didsbury, but they managed a fair degree of authenticity and, unsurprisingly, Stewart's production on both singles was spot-on. Perhaps equally unsurprisingly, neither was a hit.

The group, fearing the associations of the name Hermits was putting off potential new fans, changed their name to the suitably western Sour Mash. Though the band were proud of it, RCA declined to release the album they subsequently recorded at Pluto, putatively entitled *A Whale Of A Tale*, and Sour Mash broke up.

When the offer of re-joining Noone for a lucrative revival tour of the US arose, Leckenby,[67] Whitwam and Green

---

[66] The B-side of which was 'Effen Curly' ('Don't let 'em grab you by 'em') honest!

[67] Derek Leckenby continued with the Hermits until his untimely death on 4th June 1994. A skilled arranger and guitarist, Leckenby was always at pains to refute the idea that the band hadn't played on their hits. His reluctance to let the band's fans down by cancelling gigs during his illness hastened his demise, according to his manager.

jumped at the chance. Keith Hopwood declined, preferring to concentrate on Pluto, and he subsequently avoided the recriminations and unedifying wrangling over the rights to the name Herman's Hermits which continue to this day.[68]

---

[68] Both Noone and Whitwam have versions of the band permanently on the road. Their regular reciprocal accusations and animosity make Barney and Hooky look like Renée and Renato.

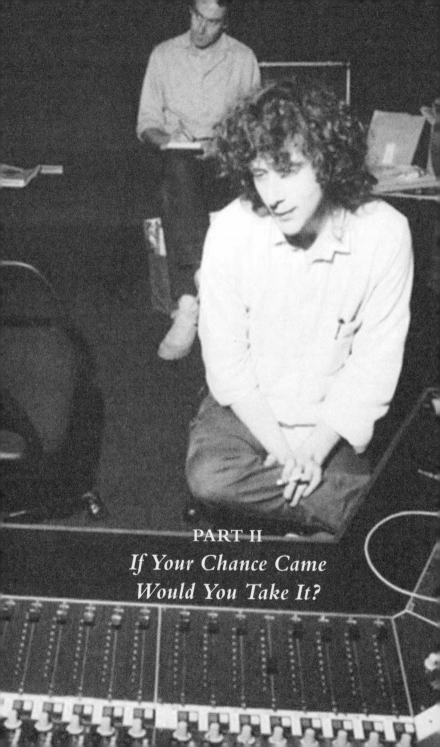

PART II
*If Your Chance Came
Would You Take It?*

Chapter 6
Lisa Take A Bow

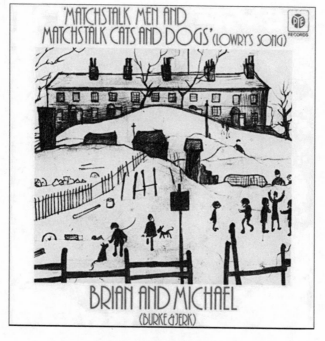

Brian and Michael
Matchstalk Men And Matchstalk Cats And Dogs

'Northern writers like to have it both ways. They set their achievements against the sometimes imaginary squalor of their origins and gain points for transcendence while at the same time implying that Northern life is richer and in some undefined way truer and more honest than a life of southern comfort. "Look, we have come through" is the stock version of it.'

– Alan Bennett, 2016

For good or ill, Manchester's unique standing in the world of music, football, art and even science is intrinsically linked – in the minds of both its proponents and those observing – to its perceived and almost mythological Northern 'attitude'. Of course, that much-discussed attitude – a dichotomous inferiority/superiority complex that is as succinctly summed up in the lyric of Graham Gouldman's 'It's Nice To Be Out In The Morning' as it is by Mr Bennett above – is shared with the rest of Northern England. It's present in the work of Newcastle's Dick Clement and Ian La Frenais. Liverpool's Alan Bleasdale and Yorkshire's David Hockney both have plenty of Northern attitude. But it has to be said, Mancunians do it particularly well. After all, they're used to having it both ways. Mancs have always balanced a justifiable pride in the city's many achievements with a simmering resentment. The resentment comes from the knowledge that those achievements – built on the sweat of the working classes – have brought massive wealth to a distinctly small minority.

'Fuck London', the simplest and most prevalent manifestation of Mancunian attitude, was there amongst the disenfranchised masses at Peterloo, and in the pages of the earliest editions of the *Manchester Guardian*.[69] It played its part in the creation of the Free Trade Hall, built on the site of the Peterloo massacre, and the formation of the Hallé Orchestra, who were based there for many years. It led John Dalton to form Manchester Mechanics' Institute,[70] and Tony Warren to create *Coronation Street*. The works of Danny Boyle have it, as does HOME, the Manchester arts centre he is patron of. As we've seen, it was absolutely central to the approach of Kennedy Street Enterprises, Harvey Lisberg in particular.[71] It motivated Eric Stewart to create Strawberry Studios, and was the guiding principle of Tony Wilson, Rob Gretton (it was pretty much his catchphrase) and Factory Records.[72]

Of course, one of the earlier, most profound, and most celebrated sightings is in the grimy landscapes of Mr Laurence Stephen Lowry.[73] And with a satisfying synchronicity, it was a significant motivator for Keith Hopwood when he created

[69] It doesn't matter that this London isn't entirely real. The fact that the elitist, greedy, insular, condescending Emerald City exists as much in the collective minds of the North as it does on the streets of the capital doesn't make its rejection any less important.

[70] Later known as UMIST (University of Manchester Institute of Science and Technology), which counts among its distinguished alumni one Martin Hannett. John Dalton, of course, was the 'father of modern atomic theory'. If that summation sounds cursory, remember you're looking for information about one of the world's greatest ever scientists in a footnote in a book about Manchester music. Give your head a wobble.

[71] It also drips off the pages of the book you hold in your hand, of course. Unfortunately *Fuck London* isn't much of a title.

[72] Wilson's oft-quoted summation of this attitude, which was slightly pithier than Mr Gretton's, was 'This is Manchester, we do things differently here'.

[73] Lowry was completely uninterested in the attentions of the London elite. Over the years he turned down an OBE, a CBE and a knighthood. A lifelong Manchester City fan, at times in the seventies he was almost as good at avoiding trips to London to collect trophies as his favourite team was.

Pluto Studios as a means to avoid the regular trek south, because what became Pluto's most successful song was a maudlin, but entirely heartfelt ballad composed as a tribute to the aforementioned Mr Lowry. It's a painfully mawkish song, yet one so heavily redolent of Manchester's artistic mythos it even elbowed its way onto the soundtrack of *24 Hour Party People*, the cinematic retelling of the Factory Records legend. It divides opinion, then, but so do the paintings of L.S. Lowry. And for both the paintings and the record, focusing on whether they're any good or not misses the point.

★

The sheer number of bands and beat groups formed in Manchester and Liverpool in the sixties meant that in order to make any kind of a living at all, many of them were forced to take up residencies in Europe. Not all of these residencies were in locations as synonymous with beat music as Hamburg of course. After traipsing round the continent's less-celebrated coffee bars, The Big Sound, a Stax-influenced six-piece from Chorlton-cum-Hardy, were forced to settle on Odense in Denmark as their base of operations. The group name was originally the less-than-glamorous The Fat Sound, but when they briefly hooked up with Manchester chanteuse Karol Keyes,[74] she refused to be described as sounding fat, and insisted they take on a less corpulent nom de voyage.

Their residency in Denmark lasted for two years, during which time they became the backing band for local legend Rock Nalle. Eventually they found it impossible to sustain a viable career, and lead guitarist Kevin Parrott and bassist

[74] Karol Keyes later became an actress under the name 'Luan Peters'. She is perhaps best known for playing the Australian guest that Basil Fawlty mistakes for a light switch in 'The Psychiatrist'. Make what you will of the fact that the same part of her anatomy gets used for a more sinister purpose in the Hammer classic *Twins of Evil*.

Michael Coleman returned to Britain separately in 1967. Kevin joined The Royal Variety Show as lead guitarist. The band went on to be the first outsiders to record at Strawberry, when Peter Tattersall sneaked them in at night to record a surreptitious demo. Kevin was still on board when the Kennedy Street-backed band changed their name to 'Oscar' and secured a deal with DJM Records, owned by Beatles publisher Dick James. He remained with the band for the next ten years.

Mick Coleman quit the music business for a time, although after a few years the bug bit him again and he began playing folk clubs as a singer-songwriter. At that time many acts on the folk scene were beginning to intersperse their work songs and sea shanties with humorous asides,[75] so Coleman duly formed a comedy-folk duo with fellow singer Brian Burke, graciously agreeing to be nicknamed 'Jerk' in the band's name.[76]

In 1977, with Manchester United set to face Liverpool in the FA Cup final, Burke and Jerk secured a one-off record deal with Philips to release 'Stretford Enders', a novelty United football song. The chant it was based on wasn't unique to United, it was sung, with minor lyrical adjustments, in pretty much every ground in the land.[77] The song they built around it was a cheery George Formbyesque ditty, with a lyric that painted football hooligans as loveable scamps, and train wrecking and mass-brawling as youthful high-jinks. Released on 6th May, it was immediately banned on local

[75] Manchester legend Mike Harding was one of the first and best-known folk acts to transform between-song banter into full-blown stand up, along with fellow Manc Bob Williamson, and the likes of Jasper Carrott, Richard Digance, Max Boyce and Billy Connolly.

[76] Well it was marginally better than 'Hare', wasn't it?

[77] 'Zigga Zagga Zigga Zagga Oi Oi Oi'. The chant originated in Germany as 'Zicke Zacke'. Some sources postulate that as it means 'to cut a goat's throat' (at a push), it was originally a dig at Italian Ultras, i.e. calling them a bunch of goat slaughterers, but this is probably false etymology.

Manchester radio[78] and subsequently failed to chart, despite the fact that two weeks later, on 21st May, United lifted the cup and scuppered Liverpool's dreams of an historic treble into the bargain.

With his hopes of chart success dashed, Mick Coleman returned to the folk clubs, where the highlight of Burke and Jerk's act was a song of Mick's celebrating the life and work of his favourite, and recently-demised, artist.[79] His lifelong love of Lowry's work had begun when he saw an original in a small gallery on Oxford Road, near the legendary Johnny Roadhouse music shop where he later bought his first guitar.[80]

Coleman's affinity with the poor and downtrodden who populated Lowry's most famous paintings was no affectation – the 'parts of Ancoats where I used to play' included Tame Street, location of one of England's last workhouses. For a time after his father deserted them, Coleman's family were among its final residents. By that time it had been rebranded a 'Public Assistance Institution' but unsurprisingly the rebadge hadn't significantly enhanced its residents' social standing. Moreover, Lowry's 'Ancoats Hospital Outpatients' Hall' depicts the very waiting room where Coleman spent the night after being the victim of a particularly vicious mugging. He ended up losing an eye.

The first time Burke and Jerk performed 'Matchstalk Men And Matchstalk Cats And Dogs' was at the Black Lion folk club in Salford, a spit-and-sawdust establishment that

[78] Personally I'd have banned it for the dreadful keyboards alone.

[79] Lowry died on 23rd February 1976.

[80] No discussion of Manchester music would be complete without a mention of Johnny Roadhouse, a jazz saxophonist and member of the Northern Variety Orchestra, who opened his famous store in 1955. Since then it has supplied several generations of Manchester musicians with new and second-hand gear. It's still there today, run by his son, also called John, and well worth a visit.

on occasion also played host to John Cooper Clarke. In the audience was Granada TV reporter Anna Ford, herself a former folksinger who had played the same clubs some years earlier, and her then-partner, producer and political activist Trevor Hyett. The oft-discussed links between the Manchester folk scene and communism were still in evidence in the seventies, though Hyett himself had recently ended his affiliation with the Communist Party over their refusal to condemn the Soviet Union's appalling human rights abuses. Nonetheless, he recognised Coleman's song as the spiritual successor to the 'Manchester Rambler', the impassioned paean to workers' freedom by Manchester folk's most famous communist son, Ewan MacColl.[81] He was also convinced of 'Matchstalk Men's commercial potential, and he and Ford urged the duo to record it as soon as possible.

Coleman approached his friend and former bandmate Kevin Parrott to produce, as he had on 'Stretford Enders'. Parrott was so taken with the song that he agreed to fund the recording himself. He'd been unimpressed with the 'Stretford Enders' recording, which was done at Dave Kent-Watson's Indigo Studios on Gartside Street,[82] so he decided that as 'Matchstalk Men' represented his best chance at producing a

[81] 'The Manchester Rambler' was written to commemorate the 1932 'Mass Trespass', which MacColl helped to organise, along with the brilliant Benny Rothman. The trespass saw 400 ramblers from Manchester and Sheffield attempt to gather on Kinder Scout, ostensibly private land. On the way, the Manchester contingent were literally read the Riot Act, 'kettled' by the local constabulary and confronted with force by the Duke of Devonshire's thuggish gamekeepers. They eventually made it, but a number of ramblers were arrested (including Rothman) and jailed for up to six months. The swingeing sentences helped turned public opinion in favour of the right to roam and Kinder later became part of the country's first national park. Roy Hattersley called it 'the most successful direct action in British history'.

[82] The studio, one of a number of smaller outfits that appeared in the wake of Strawberry's success, was opened in 1971. It was used by many of the Manchester folk acts for demo recording.

hit, it should be committed to tape at Manchester's best studio. However, he soon realised that the £1,000 he'd borrowed would struggle to cover the £25 an hour Strawberry were demanding, so he set his sights slightly lower and climbed the extra flight of stairs to Pluto, who were £9 an hour cheaper.

Financial limitations notwithstanding, Parrott had big ideas for the track. He decided that the song needed brass, not unreasonably, given the subject matter, so despite the obvious logistical issues (Pluto was only thirteen foot by thirteen) he recruited the Tintwistle Brass Band from his home village to provide it. After some ingenious furniture rearrangement he managed to cram the whole band into the tiny space and the second of the three recording sessions was spent overdubbing the plaintiff horns. Similar spatial issues presented themselves when Parrott revealed his next brainwave – a children's choir to provide harmonies on the chorus and to sing the outro, the celebrated nursery rhyme 'The Big Ship Sails On The Alley-Alley-O'.[83]

As ever, the good people down the stairs at Strawberry were on hand to help out – Peter Tattersall suggested that his daughter's school, St Winifred's, would be suitable. They were just down the road for a start, and had an experienced choir who worked under the auspices of the redoubtable Miss Terri Foley.[84] In the end, child labour laws (and limitations of

[83] Though its origins are up for debate, 'The Alley-Alley-O' is intrinsically linked, in Manchester minds at least, with the Manchester Ship Canal, the man-made waterway which allowed ocean-going vessels access to Salford and Trafford Park. Its opening in 1894 enabled Manchester businesses to sidestep the excessive tariffs imposed by Liverpool docks, and eventually the Port of Manchester became the third biggest port in the country despite being 40 miles from the sea. It understandably remains a source of immense pride in Manchester and Salford. The song is memorably sung by schoolchildren in the ultimate Northern kitchen-sink drama *A Taste of Honey.*

[84] Tattersall was struck by the St Winifred choir's charms (and marketability) and went on to produce one of Strawberry's biggest hits for them in their own right, the million-selling 'There's No One Quite Like Grandma'.

space) meant that only eight children were used and quadruple tracked.

While it's fair to say Coleman's lyric and vocals on the track struggle to negotiate the line between pride and parody, they do at least remain warm and affectionate throughout. It's particularly nice to hear 'nowt', the default Mancunian word for nothing, correctly enunciated, as it's rarely used in song. And it's true that for many, the recording paints a sound-picture that really is redolent of Lowry's best-loved art. Part of the reason for this may be that people who see the paintings after hearing the song simply see what it tells them to see. It seems unlikely that this slight pop song led many people to discover the artist, but it's difficult to find a discussion of Lowry's art online that doesn't contain the word 'matchstalk'. The word didn't really exist until Coleman put it in his lyric.

Of course the single takes an over-sentimentalised view of hardship and allows nostalgia to knock the rough edges off memory, something Lowry's paintings never do. He had little time for such indulgences. 'The thing about painting is there should be no sentiment. No sentiment,' he notably opined, and there's precious little sentimentality in works such as 'The Cripples' or the aforementioned 'Ancoats Hospital Outpatients' Hall'. But both record and paintings share a justifiable pride in basing their art in real working-class Manchester life and, sentimental or not, their subject matter remains all-but unique in both fields.[85] And even amidst his romanticism, Coleman is scathing that the art establishment's attitude remained patronising to Lowry even when they

[85] Don McLean's 'Vincent', while ostensibly covering a similar subject, is lyrically its polar opposite. McLean notes that the masses were unable and unwilling to appreciate Van Gogh's genius while 'Matchstalk Men' argues that it was ordinary folk who 'got' L.S. Lowry while the elevated art world all but ignored him.

eventually recognised his talent: 'Come on down and wear the old flat cap,' as he succinctly put it.

In the end it boils down to a single fact: Lowry's paintings spoke to Mick Coleman, and Mick returned the favour by putting L.S. Lowry higher in the public consciousness than even the artist's death the previous year had done.

With the record completed, Kevin Parrott set about securing a deal. He was still contracted to the DJM label as a member of the band Oscar, but they wouldn't touch it. Philips pronounced it 'not strong' and passed, but eventually Pye agreed to release the song, with one proviso: 'Burke and Jerk' would never do as the name of the act. They were re-christened 'Brian and Michael' and Pye geared up for a November 1977 release.

Unfortunately, with the record pressed and on its way to the shops, 'Brian and Michael' ceased to be. Brian Burke, sensing that the life of a musician with a prospective hit to promote was far removed from that of a purveyor of comic songs in obscure folk clubs, jumped ship. The extent of his involvement in the recording is debatable anyway, though he did get a songwriting credit. He returned to his ice-cream business and was never heard of again, which left Mick Coleman with a bit of an issue. Fortunately, Kevin Parrott, who knew the record had real potential and had had enough of Oscar anyway, agreed to become a new Brian.

The song hit the shops on 25th November and slowly began to gain traction in the New Year. However, when it reached No. 45, it was briefly suspended from the charts amidst accusations of hyping, due to the inevitable bias of Northern sales. Once it was ascertained that sales were genuine, Mick and Kevin, or rather Brian and Michael, were asked to appear on *Top of the Pops*, sitting cloth-capped amidst a stereotypically dreary generic 'Northern' backdrop. Whoever designed the set was probably unfamiliar with what Manchester really looked like as *Top of the Pops* had upped sticks and moved to London in 1966. It was a sensible decision, as most of the artists who appeared on the programme had done the same thing.

Unwilling to pay for St Winifred's choir to come to the capital for the TV appearance, the BBC instead summoned Miss Foley. She did her best to instruct local schoolchildren in the art of Northern pronunciation, but the resultant vocals were inevitably rather more 'ecky thump' than on the original. Lowry's cheerier paintings were interspersed with the visuals and demand for prints rose immediately.

The single continued to climb the charts in the spring and by the time it reached No. 1 on 4th April 1978 it was selling 60,000 copies a day. It spent three weeks at the top of the charts and sold over a million copies. Mick Coleman received an Ivor Novello award for 'Outstanding Lyric Of The Year', beating 'Don't Cry For Me Argentina' into the bargain.

Kevin and Mick never repeated its success, of course. The follow-up single, 'Evensong', a quasi-religious dirge foisted on them by Pye, did nothing. It was far too removed from 'Matchstalk Men' to effectively ride on its coattails, even though it did boast the requisite choir and brass. Their preferred choice, a song they'd written themselves called 'Mam When's Mi Dad Coming Home? (The Dream)' was more in keeping, but by the time they released that it was too late. Brian and Michael released two albums, but had no further hits. They did however produce novelty hits for two other sets of Manchester school kids: The Ramblers[86] from Gorton's Abbey Hey School, and Claire and Friends, another St Winifred's effort. This one featured 9-year-old Claire

[86] 'The Sparrow' (UK No. 11, 1979)

Usher, who came to the attention of the public by winning a *Saturday Superstore* talent competition with the song.[87]

Besides raising the profile of L.S. Lowry, the runaway success of 'Matchstalk Men And Matchstalk Cats And Dogs' had a similar effect on Pluto Studios, and for the first time it was flagged as a viable venue for producing big hits. This raised awareness came at a particularly apposite time too, as Keith Hopwood was about to realise a long-held dream to relocate the studio to the centre of Manchester. He'd known for some time that as long as Pluto was located upstairs at Waterloo Road, it would inevitably play second fiddle to the state-of the-art facility below. Added to that, he realised that as most of the studio's commercial recordings were being ferried to Granada on Quay Street the minute they were recorded, it made sense to stop travelling eight miles up the A6 every time.

Hopwood had been scouting for a prospective new home all year and with singular good fortune he eventually found an empty facility on Granby Row, just off Whitworth Street, and not far from Piccadilly. Consisting mainly of ex-textile warehouses and university faculties, in many ways the buildings on Granby Row represented Manchester's evolution in microcosm, so it's fitting that they also housed a facility for the city's other major export: music. Within three years Pluto Manchester would play host to many iconic acts, including The Clash and The Fall, and also served as the birthplace for one of Manchester's most celebrated records, the eponymous debut album by The Smiths.

---

[87] 'It's 'Orrible Being In Love (When You're 8½)' (UK No. 13, 1986). I have no wish to cast aspersions on the legitimacy of said talent contest, but how many of the other entrants had songs custom-written by Ivor Novello award winners?

Chapter 7
A Silly Phase

10cc
I'm Not In Love

Strawberry's musicians had spent a year or so more or less happily rolling turds in glitter, but it was blindingly obvious that such activities were never going to satisfactorily scratch their collective artistic itch.[88] Wisely, they decided that what they needed was a chance to work with a real recording artist with proper artistic ambitions, all the while remaining blissfully unaware that between the four of them they constituted exactly that. Charged with finding such an act, Harvey Lisberg somehow managed to secure Neil Sedaka.[89] Lisberg engineered a 'chance' meeting with the veteran singer-songwriter in New York, and got to work. It was no small task, convincing one of the sixties' most successful composers that working in an unheard of studio nestled between Stockport's dank satanic mills was just what he needed. On top of that, of course, Lisberg had to persuade him to work with an anonymous quartet rather than top-class session musicians. However, when Sedaka expressed a grudging admiration for Strawberry's bubblegum recording 'There Ain't No Umbopo' Lisberg seized his chance. He pointed out that Tony Christie's

[88] They did produce and play on one slightly more cerebral record at this time: comedian John Paul Jones's 'The Man From Nazareth'. The single, which owed a fairly heavy debt to Jimmy Dean's 'Big Bad John', looked like being a decent Christmas hit until Jones parted company with Harvey Lisberg and was subsequently banned from using the name John Paul Jones by Led Zeppelin's management. This forced a re-release under the barely different alias of John Paul Joans and the break in momentum meant it never got higher than No. 25. Perhaps he should have stuck with 'Reg Davidge'.

[89] Sedaka enjoyed massive success as a singer/songwriter in the fifties and sixties. One of his best-known tunes 'Oh Carol' was written in honour of Carole King, one half of the Goffin–King songwriting team who provided many songs to Herman's Hermits, The Mindbenders et al.

'Is This The Way To Amarillo', which had given Sedaka his first hit as a songwriter in years, had actually also been recorded in Stockport. Incredibly, the Brill Building stalwart not only agreed to come to Manchester to record, but he also allowed Strawberry joint artistic control of the sessions.

Sedaka first walked Stockport's damp streets in February 1972, and subsequently recorded a full album there: *Solitaire*, the title reflecting his status as a stranger in a strange land. The doom-laden title track, with its palpable air of Northern misery, would go on to be a huge hit for both Andy Williams and The Carpenters. Neil himself would hit the charts again as an artist for the first time in seven years when 'That's When The Music Takes Me' was released as a single. It was clear that Sedaka's stay in Manchester had reignited his creative fires.

Everyone involved was sufficiently pleased with the results that they jumped at the chance to do it all again, once the Strawberry musicians had negotiated more financial recompense than the flat session fees they'd received the first time. For Sedaka, moving from his comfort zone to the soot-streaked streets of Manchester had put him back in touch with his hit making instincts. For the four Manchester musicians, working on a whole album's worth of serious material was a massive relief from churning out endless standalone novelty hits.[90] The second Sedaka album produced at Strawberry was called *The Tra-La Days Are Over*,[91] which used an ironic

[90] The other major album project they worked on at the time was the bonkers-prog epic *Space Hymns* by Ramases, who was the actual reincarnation of the Egyptian Pharaoh Ramesses II. Until revealing this to the world, he'd been biding his time as a central heating fitter in Sheffield called Kimberley Barrington-Frost.

[91] The line is taken from the song 'This Will Be Our Last Song Together' which simultaneously represented and memorialised the ending of his partnership with lyricist Howard Greenfield. Neil had written some of his best-known hits with Greenfield and the resultant performance is remarkably raw, and achingly authentic. Sedaka sounds on the verge of tears throughout.

reference to the hook of his 1961 hit 'Happy Birthday Sweet Sixteen' to signal its sombre and melancholic mood. Even the stand out track from the album, which went on to be a massive hit for Captain & Tennille, tempered Sedaka's cautious optimism with palpable insecurity. The title of the song, 'Love Will Keep Us Together', would later provide direct inspiration for Ian Curtis, who used a cracked mirror image as the chorus of his greatest and most poignant lyric: 'Love Will Tear Us Apart'. With unbelievable synchronicity, and unbeknownst to Curtis at the time, both tales of the underlying paranoia lurking beneath a long-term relationship were recorded in the same room.[92]

In the end, working with Sedaka had a profound effect on the four musicians. They'd had a taste of what it would be like to be an actual functioning band once before: the 'Neanderthal Man' single had led to Hotlegs and Gouldman playing some support slots for the Moody Blues, but that identity had fizzled out almost as quickly as the imaginary bands they pretended to be for Kasenetz-Katz. Over a late-night Chinese meal, the four of them realised that recording some decent material of their own was the way to go. Recording crap like 'Susan's Tuba' was all very diverting, and even lucrative, but it was high time they explored what they could do with a song they actually believed in.

The first song the as-yet unnamed band recorded was 'Waterfall', a back-to-the country ballad in the style of America or Crosby, Stills, Nash and Young.[93] It only really transcends its ersatz origins for the remarkable backwards instrumental

[92] Malcolm McLaren later put together a remix which merges the two songs, albeit the Captain & Tennille version.

[93] Though seen as the archetypal US vocal supergroup, CSN&Y were in fact a quarter Salfordian. It comprised David Crosby from The Byrds, Stephen Stills and Neil Young of Buffalo Springfield, and The Hollies' Graham Nash.

section, which arrives completely out of the blue, messes with the whole fabric of the song and then disappears. In fact the recording's combination of old-fashioned songwriting with try-anything production techniques set the blueprint for everything they would go on to create together.

Eric's first instinct was to take 'Waterfall' to Apple, who immediately and unceremoniously rejected it as 'not commercial enough'. It didn't matter, as the song they recorded for the B-side, 'Donna', a self-conscious doo-wop pastiche with a ridiculous falsetto, was obviously more commercial anyway.[94] 'Donna' was a decidedly odd beast though, and the quartet decided that the best person to send it to would be another decidedly odd beast, Jonathan King,[95] who Eric Stewart had known since the Mindbender days. It took one listen over the phone to convince King of the song's commerciality and he headed straight up to Stockport.

If nothing else, King did two things that forged the dissolute foursome into a real functioning band. Firstly, he gave them the all but meaningless name 10cc.[96] Secondly, he decided that the best image for the studious and studio-based quartet was no image at all. Like the Mancunian punk bands that would follow them in 1976, 10cc would take to the stage in the clothes they'd been in all day.[97]

[94] They may have fared better taking that song to Apple, as *Abbey Road*'s 'Oh! Darling' was a notably similar doo-wop tribute.

[95] Jonathan King was the master of marketing novelty records, e.g. The Piglets' 'Johnny Reggae'; 'Leap Up And Down (Wave Your Knickers In The Air)' by St Cecelia; Terry Dactyl & The Dinosaurs' 'Seaside Shuffle' and 'Loop Di Love' by the 'hilariously' named Shag.

[96] The name came to him in a dream and, despite popular legend, had no links whatsoever to the substance referenced in the band names of The Lovin' Spoonful and Pearl Jam.

[97] This was one of the really significant differences between the London punk bands and their Manchester counterparts. While the Sex Pistols advertised Vivienne

The group signed to King's UK record label and rationalised their organisation by making Harvey Lisberg and Ric Dixon co-managers of the band. In October 1972, 'Donna' went to No. 2 in the UK, but the follow-up, 'Johnny Don't Do It' did absolutely nothing. Perhaps understandably, given the success of its predecessor, 'Johnny Don't Do It' was another pastiche, this time of the motorbike-death keens of the Shangri-Las and their ilk. With hindsight, it was probably a good thing for the band that it failed to chart, as they may well have continued to write novelty period pieces forever.

Instead, they hit on a unique musical formula, one that owed everything to the unprecedented way the band came into being. It successfully blended their talent for melody and commerciality with enough knowing winks to keep the band sufficiently amused and stimulated. Consequently there's never really been another band like 10cc.[98] Maintaining such a fine balance was a constant battle, but whether you see it as a battle between simplicity and erudition, or over-earnestness and smart-arsedness, depends on your opinion of the group. Either way, their third single 'Rubber Bullets' got the balance just about right. It combined a lyric that pointed out that the events of 'Jailhouse Rock' probably wouldn't have ended as well as Elvis made out, with a marvellous guitar solo recorded at half-speed. It reached No. 1 in the UK and even broke into the US Hot 100.

Westwood, The Clash spray-painted situationist slogans on their jumpsuits and the Damned raided the fancy dress shop, Buzzcocks, Joy Division and The Fall resembled nothing so much as low-paid office workers onstage, which of course Mark E. Smith and Ian Curtis actually were.

[98] Perhaps the nearest equivalent was Steely Dan, whose sound was a similar marriage of art and commerciality. Their output was far more jazz influenced however and consequently even more smart-arsed. Eric Stewart was obsessed with Steely Dan's 'dry studio sound' and sought to create a similar set up at Strawberry. His ambition was to be able to record instruments with no natural ambience and allow the producer to build their own synthesised 'room' from scratch.

Their next release 'The Dean And I' possibly veered a little bit too far into clever-clever territory, being a note-perfect Brian Wilson/Rogers and Hammerstein pastiche (that word again). As a production it's genuinely startling, and the record is certainly admirable, but it sacrifices a deal of its likeability on the altar of self-conscious musicality. Eric Stewart, for one, hated it. That said, it was a pretty big hit, which is more than can be said for their next two releases. 'Headline Hustler' and 'The Worst Band In The World' were perfectly adequate album tracks but should never have been released as singles. Luckily their next release, 'The Wall Street Shuffle', was their best to date by far. A distant cousin to 'Money' by Pink Floyd, both musically and lyrically, it's catchy piano run later turned up on the similarly fiscally-obsessed 'Money Money Money' by Abba. It returned them to the singles charts where they remained undisturbed for the next three years. Most satisfyingly of all, the pinnacle of this chart success, which came in May 1975, coincided with their ultimate artistic achievement. A marriage of brilliant songwriting and exquisite production that has seldom been bettered, 'I'm Not In Love' owes its very existence to the fact that the band had their own studio to play with.

It was written by Stewart and Gouldman for the band's third album, *The Original Soundtrack*. Even in its original incarnation as a slow bossa-nova, it's obvious that 'I'm Not In Love' is a brilliant song. Obvious to everyone but Kevin Godley anyway. 'It's crap,' was his considered opinion. In fact it was his disdain for the original arrangement that spurred him to the game-changing idea for the vocal instrumentation. Had he stuck to his guns, and refused to work on the song, it would never have seen the light of day: each member of the band had the power of veto on every song. He was clearly wrong in his opinion though. Lyrically, the way 'I'm

Not In Love' leaves the subtext to the listener is especially satisfying, and all the more poignant for it. Musically, the chord progression fits the lyric like a glove and leaves just enough space for its supressed emotionality. It's so self-evidently complete that no act who was paying the producer and the studio by the hour would ever have taken the time to furnish it with one of rock music's greatest productions. What's more, only a band who had obliterated the division between performer, engineer, producer and studio owner could have done it the way 10cc did.[99]

The only other seventies single which could even attempt to match its bonkers multi-tracked excess was Queen's 'Bohemian Rhapsody', released the same year. However, that track's time-consuming and costly multi-tracking was arguably part of the composition process.[100] Shorn of its studio trickery, 'Bohemian Rhapsody' barely constitutes a song at all. 10cc spent three weeks recording and bouncing tracks to create a vocal orchestra that was fully playable via the mixing desk because they could, and for their own diversion. 'I'm Not In Love' didn't need it.

But thank goodness they did. Every bizarre and seemingly unwarranted piece of production magic, from its out of phase plastic music box and Gouldman's decidedly *outré* bass solo to Strawberry receptionist Kathy Redfern's breathy words of reassurance, totally justifies its inclusion. The instrumentation is so appropriate to the track's air of wistful commitment-phobia that it can't be unheard – all subsequent cover versions

[99] Strawberry had replaced its 'Neanderthal Man'-funded 8-track machine with a 16-track, financed by the profits of 10cc's second album, immediately prior to recording the track. Even so, it required some distinctly imaginative Heath Robinson tape manipulation to accommodate the eventual 624(!) tracks of vocals.

[100] When it was released 'Bohemian Rhapsody' was widely acknowledged as the most expensive single of all time.

and attempts to strip the song back to traditional instruments sound just plain wrong, including the ill-advised one by Stewart and Gouldman in 1995. There can be no greater testament to the groundbreaking production than that. Released as a single in May 1975 it reached No. 1 in the UK and No. 2 in the US, the only US Top 10 the original quartet ever had. It has a permanent place on US radio, and when film soundtracks require an emotive track to put the viewer in the right place and time it's usually the first name on the list. 10cc never bettered it.

In a roundabout way, the song contributed to the break-up of the band. Prior to recording *The Original Soundtrack*, when it became clear that Jonathan King's label didn't have the clout to market it sufficiently, the group signed a massive deal with Phonogram. Though Stewart and Creme favoured Virgin, Lisberg and Dixon went with the best deal, rather than what they saw as the vague promises of a middle-class southern hippy with one successful album under his belt. Consequently the group, though a little aggrieved, was awash with cash. Furthermore, partly because the production on 'I'm Not In Love' was such a revelation, Strawberry was booked solid and they were struggling to get time in their own studio. They eventually managed to record their next album, *How Dare You!*, there, but the sessions were unsatisfyingly sporadic, though they did yield two sizeable hits. The first was 'Art For Art's Sake', which took an old aphorism Graham learned from his father and turned it into an art-rocker somewhat reminiscent of John Lennon's 'Cold Turkey'. The second was the distinctly Beatlesque 'I'm Mandy Fly Me'. Both songs did very well,[101] at least in the UK, considering their manifestly ambitious and challenging structures.

---

[101] UK No. 5 and 6 respectively. The US had a harder time accepting the two singles' wayward pop, and they only reached 83 and 60 on the Billboard chart.

Strawberry's profits continued to be ploughed back into its infrastructure, and at this point the band decided collectively to use some of their surplus assets to build a second studio for their own exclusive use. They also took the fateful decision to locate the studio away from Stockport, eventually deciding on Dorking, where they could be nearer to their musical friends who had relocated down south years ago. If Strawberry was their gift to Manchester, then Strawberry South was their gift to themselves. As it turned out, the original line-up of 10cc never recorded a note there.

The band simply wasn't big enough to contain the ambitions of all its members. Graham Gouldman's aspirations were completely served by 10cc – he was finally a member of a successful band who both encouraged and improved his songwriting. And opening a sister studio had effectively accommodated Eric Stewart's plans to continue to improve Strawberry Stockport and still allow them time to record. But it turned out Godley and Creme's technological ambitions weren't so easily reconciled. Years earlier, in conjunction with John McConnell at UMIST, they had invented a device they christened 'Gizmo', which fitted to a guitar and used battery-driven rotors to allow infinite sustain. What's more, unlike its predecessor the e-bow, it could be used on multiple strings at once.

They decided that they now had sufficient financial acumen and spare cash to attempt to mass market it. However, it soon became clear that using the Gizmo correctly required a degree of dedication and a delicacy of touch most guitarists lacked, so it was never going to achieve mass appeal. As Godley memorably put it: 'It wasn't plug-and-play, it was plug-and-fuck-around-for-three-days.' Still, by this stage Godley and Creme were obsessed with it. After using it on a few 10cc tracks[102] they decided that the best way to showcase the device was to release an album completely based around it. With a megalomania not entirely uncommon amongst seventies studio-based artists, they eventually recorded *Consequences*, a triple concept album, incorporating a play and a spoken word section voiced by Peter Cook. It was overlong, over-egged and over-ambitious. It was also, for want of a better word, a bit boring. Unfortunately it hit the shops in 1977, just as punk's seismic shift was hitting the music industry: 'boring' was the worst thing you could possibly be, and triple albums were first to the bonfire. Godley and Creme had dug their own grave. Literally, at one point – to give the listener the impression that they were being buried alive, they put a mic in a box and recorded it being covered in sand.[103] The album suffered the same fate as the Gizmo itself, both now remembered only as expensive curios with no lasting impact at all.

Except one. Having thrown their everything into the grand folly that was the Gizmo (or 'Gizmotron' as it was to be marketed) Creme and Godley had effectively moved so far into the avant-garde that they lost interest in pop music all together. They could hear no merit at all in 'The Things We Do For Love', a charming Stewart-Gouldman composition that was slated for 10cc's next single and, unlike with 'I'm Not In Love', had no intention of working on it. The band split in two, and Stewart and Gouldman took over the name.[104]

As their wives were sisters, the less-than-amicable split put a considerable strain on Stewart and Creme's family life for

---

[102] E.g. 'Baron Samedi' and 'Brand New Day'.

[103] I'm sure it was worth it.

[104] Eric Stewart later expressed the opinion that possession of the name 10cc was the only reason Gouldman stayed with him.

the next few years. Musically though, at least initially, the separation was helpful. Stewart and Gouldman released the next 10cc album *Deceptive Bends* to some critical acclaim. Its simpler structure was somewhat vindicated when 'The Things We Do For Love' reached No. 6 in the UK and No. 5 in the US, which was the highest the duo ever got in America. That vindication was a two-edged sword of course, as it meant neither of them would ever feel the need to work as hard on a song again as they had for 'I'm Not In Love'. The band had two more major hits, 'Good Morning Judge' and 'Dreadlock Holiday', one of those rare songs that completely polarises opinion.[105]

In January 1979, Eric suffered an horrendous car crash. He lost the sight in one eye and his hearing was so badly affected he was forced to abandon music for a year, during which time Gouldman scored what was, incredibly, his first solo hit, 'Sunburn'.[106] After Stewart's convalescence 10cc soldiered on, but neither Stewart's nor Gouldman's heart was really in it.

Once Creme and Godley had returned to their senses and abandoned the psychosis of triple albums and unsaleable technology, it was inevitable that they'd get back to making thoughtful pop, and in 1981 they had a couple of sizeable UK hits.[107] Almost as an afterthought, they quietly revolutionised the music industry again, when they all but invented music video in the 1980s. They introduced elements into the

[105] 'Dreadlock Holiday' tells the exact same first-hand story as 'Safe European Home' by The Clash. Two English rock stars head to Jamaica to sample reggae culture and during their first trip downtown are so frightened by the local scene they spend the rest of their holiday by the hotel pool. You get the impression that Stewart and Gouldman enjoyed the experience more than Strummer and Jones though. Maybe it was the piña coladas, or the fact that Joe and Mick had no suitable clothing. They must have been boiling in those leather jackets.

[106] From the film of the same name. It reached No. 52 in June 1979.

[107] 'Under Your Thumb' (No. 3) and 'Wedding Bells' (No. 7).

videos they directed that became industry standards almost overnight. These included stop-motion, in Visage's 'Fade To Grey'; image cross-fading, for their own 'Cry'; the band as extras in their own video, for Frankie Goes to Hollywood's 'Two Tribes'; and soft porn, for Duran Duran's 'Girls On Film'. Mixtures of the last two proved especially popular, for obvious reasons.

A half-hearted attempt by Polydor to reunite the four original members of 10cc in 1991 resulted in what was effectively a Gouldman-Stewart album with some Kevin Godley and Lol Creme backing vocals. A distinctly lacklustre affair, it sank without trace, but the band limped on minus Godley and Creme before finally calling it a day in 1995. As of 2017, Gouldman leads a touring version of 10cc, much to Stewart's chagrin, and the original group have again split into two factions. Gouldman and Godley occasionally work together as GG/06; Stewart and Creme remain friends and brothers-in-law.

The band's ignominious ending is a shame, as is the fact that they remain relatively uncelebrated when compared to such contemporary bands as Queen or Fleetwood Mac. If the achievements of the four members of 10cc are bracketed together, they are truly staggering. Between them they wrote and performed several of the most successful songs of the sixties, enjoyed massive success in the seventies as both a singles and albums band, created one of the decade's most innovative and much-loved records, and kick-started the music video revolution of the eighties. On top of that, and arguably even more importantly, they bequeathed Manchester a proper world-class recording facility that was affordable even to impoverished independent labels.

Chapter 8
It Seems So Real

Buzzcocks
Everybody's Happy Nowadays

The gigs that many view as Manchester music's big bang – the two performances at the Lesser Free Trade Hall by the Sex Pistols in June and July of 1976 – were organised by the nascent Buzzcocks. Bolton Institute students Pete Shelley and Howard Devoto, and their friend Richard Boon who would go on to be the band's manager, were intrigued and excited by what they'd read in the *NME* about the Sex Pistols. They were determined to witness this new phenomenon for themselves and, given the Pistols' limited touring circuit, they had no option but to travel to London to see them, so that's what they did. As impressed as they were by the two performances they witnessed,[108] they had neither the desire nor the financial wherewithal to keep making the journey south in order to see the band play. What's more they wanted to give other Mancunians a chance to see Johnny Rotten in all his glory, so they decided to bring the Sex Pistols to Manchester. Of course, this decision wasn't entirely selfless – they had aspirations for their own group (once they'd got round to forming it) to support the Pistols – but it did have echoes of the birth of Strawberry and Pluto. A Mancunian with vision asked 'Why does it have to be in London?' and triggered the events that meant it didn't.

The two gigs that followed have rightly achieved legendary status. Buzzcocks weren't ready to play the first concert at the Lesser Free Trade Hall,[109] but they put it on

[108] High Wycombe College 20th February 1976 and Welwyn Garden City the following night.

[109] Their truncated first gig at Bolton Institute on 1st April was enough to convince them they were nowhere near good enough.

anyway, with the entirely inappropriate Solstice as support.[110] It's impossible to say whether Peter Hook, Bernard Sumner, Mark E. Smith, Morrissey and the rest would have gone on to form the seminal bands they did if they hadn't all breathed the same tobacco-filled air that June evening – but thanks to Shelley and Devoto we don't have to. Because of their efforts, Manchester's leading lights witnessed the Sex Pistols and either thought 'this band is brilliant – I should do that'; 'this band is terrible – I could do that', or more likely some indefinable combination of the two. When Alan Wrigley witnessed The Beatles in Urmston in 1963, their sheer professionalism and other-worldliness convinced him he could never emulate them. Somehow the Sex Pistols had the exact opposite effect on their audience, and in the six weeks between that gig and a hastily arranged follow-up at the same venue, a new Manchester music scene was born. Buzzcocks were fully formed by the time of the second gig, thanks to the arrival of Steve Diggle on bass – who they actually hooked up with at the first Pistols show – and sixteen-year-old John Maher on drums. They put themselves third on the bill, below Wythenshawe glam upstarts Slaughter and the Dogs.[111]

As well as kick-starting this entirely new Mancunian musical movement, Buzzcocks were to some degree responsible for the national one that followed (fairly) soon after. At some point Devoto managed to get the Sex Pistols demo that Malcolm McLaren had given him to Tony Wilson, who not only came

[110] The highlight of their set was a cover of Mountain's 'Nantucket Sleighride', best known in the UK at that time as the theme tune of LWT's *Weekend World*.

[111] As someone who (proudly) grew up there I can categorically state that there are few greater triumphs of optimism over experience than a glam band from Wythenshawe. There's nothing very 'glam' about Civic Centre, believe me.

to the Lesser Free Trade Hall gig but gave them a slot on his seminal TV show *So It Goes*,[112] their first exposure on national TV, a full three months before their infamous appearance on Bill Grundy's *Today* show.

But Buzzcocks had another seismic achievement up their sleeves. *Spiral Scratch*, their initially unassuming debut EP, released a mere six months after their debut performance, inspired another revolution. In short, it had the same effect on the record industry as the Sex Pistols gigs at the Lesser Free Trade had on their Manchester audience. Every would-be musician who picked up *Spiral Scratch* realised that this was something they could do themselves. The reason Buzzcocks put their own record out was because they had no choice. Though it was now possible to record in Manchester, the major labels were still as reluctant to travel north to seek out talent as they had been fifteen years earlier when they'd harvested their artists from the denizens of Soho's coffee bars. The band, who prided themselves on their distance from the London elite, were in no mood to up sticks and join it. Not yet anyway.

Buzzcocks borrowed £500 from their friends and family, which paid for four tracks to be recorded at Manchester's Indigo studios. By Christmas 1976, when *Spiral Scratch* was committed to tape, Indigo's main sources of income were folk acts recording demos and pop artists re-recording their hits. The Musicians' Union, in their wisdom, had decided that it was cheating if acts just mimed to their singles on TV, but as most shows (including *Top of the Pops*) weren't equipped for live performance they demanded hastily re-recorded versions.

[112] Of course, the Pistols' appearance is one of the main reasons it's considered seminal.

In Indigo's case the main customers were Granada's *Lift Off With Ayshea*[113] and *Shang-a-Lang*.[114]

The Buzzcocks' session was engineered by in-house engineer Phil Hampson, and produced by Martin Hannett, or 'Martin Zero' as he styled himself at the time. Hannett may well have been destined to become one of Britain's most acclaimed producers, but he only got the gig through proximity – he ran a gig agency from the same building that Buzzcocks had their office.

In keeping with the band's egalitarian nature, each member picked one song each from their set to record. The resultant EP was a hastily produced piece of would-be vérité. It wasn't really successful in achieving Hannett's professed ambition to capture the sound of the band onstage (it was a bit tinny for that), but it was close enough. The four tracks ('Boredom', 'Friends Of Mine', 'Time's Up', and 'Breakdown') became the stuff of Manchester legend, and perennial mainstays of the band's live set.

Buzzcocks created a record label, which they dubbed 'New Hormones', in order to release the EP themselves. They paid Phonogram to press the discs and packaged the thousand records themselves in a simple black and white sleeve. Rough Trade in London agreed to stock and distribute it and the initial pressing sold out almost immediately. The record was continually re-pressed until it eventually shifted 16,000 copies. The major success of *Spiral*

[113] Presented by Ayshea Brough, one of the first Asian women to front a UK TV show, who later married CBS president Michael Levy. It was a children's version of *Top of the Pops* which also featured Wally Whyton, a singer and graduate of the 2is Coffee Bar, and Ollie Beak, an owl. The episode me, Marc Riley and my brother Steve attended in July 1974 featured The Rockin' Berries, Paul Da Vinci and Barry Blue. Like the artists discussed above, I like to think that this early exposure to rock and roll was what later made us all join bands.

[114] The dismal Bay City Rollers-fronted follow-up to *Lift Off*.

Scratch was that it showed that a cheap self-released record was viable, and that it was possible to reach an audience without the involvement of a major record company. Many observers credit *Spiral Scratch* with being the catalyst for the entire 'independent record label' ethos. Certainly, Rough Trade boss Geoff Travis added a record label to his shop and distribution business soon after.

For reasons that he never satisfactorily explained, Howard Devoto left the band just as the record was released. Though the split was infinitely more amicable than the one between Wayne Fontana and The Mindbenders, Buzzcocks dealt with the departure of their equally charismatic lead singer in much the same way. Pete Shelley was more than happy to take on the frontman role, and in truth he was even more suited to it than Devoto. With Shelley's lovelorn vocal stylings front and centre, and Steve Diggle on second guitar, a new and uniquely thrilling sound emerged – the real Buzzcocks sound – and their momentum didn't falter for a second.

Buzzcocks had plans for a second independent EP, which they planned to call *Love Bites*. However, John Maher's father rightly pointed out that this plan would leave them with nothing to live on for the foreseeable future. The band decided it would be more financially prudent to take the London shilling.

Of course, once 'punk' became the next big thing, the record labels had to grit their teeth and seek out bands the length and breadth of the country. In theory, punk came with an air of authenticity distinctly lacking in previous musical movements, so the labels started out by looking for real proponents of this new musical form. But once they realised that the record-buying public weren't really that bothered about authenticity and preferred a good tune, they immediately stopped seeking out real punk bands and started rebranding more socially acceptable acts. Hence 'new wave'.

Buzzcocks signed to United Artists on 16th August 1977, the day Elvis Presley died. Diggle used his part of the advance to buy a 1959 Gibson Les Paul Jnr guitar that the man in the shop assured him had once belonged to Tony Hicks from The Hollies. Hicks later confirmed as much to him when they met in the studio. 'We're the Buzzcocks and we're from Manchester, too. I'm taking this guitar on to the next phase,' Diggle told the man who had played on twenty-seven UK Top 30 hits and six US Top 10s. In what was surely the musical equivalent of 'Billy's Boots',[115] Diggle went on to play it on every Buzzcocks recording session till the band split.

Their first single for United Artists was the Devoto-penned 'Orgasm Addict'. It had always been earmarked as their next release, back when the tracks for *Spiral Scratch* were decided. The band used its provocative title as a bargaining tool when determining how serious record companies were about signing them. An otherwise infectious pop song, the lyric, and certainly the title, had more than a hint of punk's tendency to be deliberately controversial just to wind up the straights. That said, it displayed a deal more wit and humour than wearing a swastika armband ever did.

The last remaining songs from their Devoto set list were swiftly dispatched on their first album *Another Music In A Different Kitchen*[116] and from that point Shelley's songwriting was in the ascendance. Even then the songs that he'd written alone

[115] Classic seventies comic strip, usually featured in the *Tiger*. Seeing as how Dead-Shot Keen's footy boots had such a profound effect on his game, you'd think Billy would have taken better care of them; they were nicked or lost every other week. To underline the similarities, the guitar was stolen from Diggle immediately after Buzzcocks broke up.

[116] 'Fast Cars', 'Love Battery', 'You Tear Me Up'.

were better than the Devoto–Shelley numbers, and any drop in intellectualism in the lyrics was more than replaced by heartfelt authenticity. The album was a brilliant debut. Shelley, as always, had an ingenious knack for simultaneously celebrating and subverting the very idea of the love song, and Diggle's 'Autonomy' was quite possibly the best song he ever wrote for the band. Maher turned in a near perfect performance, as did new bassist Steve Garvey. They both had a real knack of adding brilliantly inventive enhancements that never overshadowed the songs. Shelley and Diggle were lucky to have them.

For a time, Shelley revelled in his role as the band's main singer–songwriter, and the band produced by far its best work when he was in almost sole charge. From 'What Do I Get?' to 'Promises'[117] via 'I Don't Mind', 'Love You More' and their biggest hit 'Ever Fallen In Love...?' Shelley delivered a near flawless string of classic pop love songs. The songs he composed for their second album *Love Bites* were at least the equal of the ones on *Another Music*, and with 'Nostalgia' and 'Sixteen Again' he showed himself to be every bit as accomplished a lyricist as Howard Devoto. Eventually the pressure of this compositional heavy-lifting proved too much, and Steve Diggle's songwriting quotient was promoted from one song an album to all-but parity to make up the shortfall. Unfortunately, the increase in the quantity of Diggle's output wasn't always matched in quality.

The band's motivation for recording their next single after 'Promises' at Strawberry had more to do with a desire to spend some time at home after a frantic two years, than any desire to re-connect with their spiritual forebears. They hadn't recorded

[117] Diggle wrote the music for 'Promises', though he was clearly attempting to emulate Shelley's style (which he actually did quite convincingly).

anything in Manchester since *Spiral Scratch* and were usually happy for Martin Rushent to choose the studio. More often than not this meant Olympic Studios in the London Borough of Richmond upon Thames. When the band insisted, Rushent reluctantly agreed to make the trip north.

Recording on home soil was an important decision though, as the band were really quite frazzled by this point. The last two years had consisted of non-stop gigging and recording, and relations between the band members were increasingly fractious, as they inevitably are in such circumstances. With hindsight, it's clear that what they most needed was a break. But, as with many musicians who seemingly rely on their imaginations to make a living, they showed a distinct lack of it when it came to seeking diversions beyond the Buzzcocks bubble. John Maher began playing drums with The Things[118] and Steve Garvey played bass with The Teardrops.[119] Shelley continued to make electronic music both alone and with The Tiller Boys. Had they never heard of golf?

When they gathered at Strawberry on the 27th January 1979, they knew what their next single would be. As it turned out, it represented the peak of Shelley's songwriting dominance. Lyrically he was beginning to look beyond songs of love and heartbreak and seeking to address his growing sense of purposelessness. 'Everybody's Happy Nowadays', a title dripping with irony, was actually taken from Aldous Huxley's *Brave New World*. In the book the main character, convinced that it's impossible to be truly happy in a world without the freedom to be unhappy, ends up taking his own life. Heady

[118] Manchester-based garage band who did great versions of 'Baby Please Don't Go' and 'Walking In The Sand'. They actually supported Buzzcocks on their ill-fated 1980 'Tour By Instalments' with Maher playing two sets.

[119] The band also featured Martin Bramah and Karl Burns, soon to be ex-members of The Fall, though both would later rejoin.

stuff for a 3-minute pop song, and it gives the lie to the off-repeated idea that Shelley wrote fluff.[120] 'Love is a dream', he'd decided, which must have been a painful discovery. After all, he'd seemed pretty convinced of its existence over the course of the last two albums and five singles. From this point on, his relentless soul-searching ceased to be a useful tool to push him to greater lyrical insight and began to look more and more like evidence of a damaged psyche. His growing propensity for self-medication didn't help either.

Musically, 'Everybody's Happy Nowadays' did little to highlight the irony in the lyric, apart from Shelley's dissonant rhythm guitar, which was mixed low anyway. Without a doubt this was deliberate, as Shelley was never one for talking down to his audience. He probably expected people to work out that the jaunty melody actually concealed a cry for help. For the most part, they didn't. It's hardly surprising, as the rest of the band embellished the song with a marvellous, if inappropriately buoyant, rhythm section, and a lead guitar part as jolly as an ice-cream van's chimes.

The B-side of the single, also recorded at Strawberry, was a co-write between the four members of the band, something that only happened one other time.[121] They had gathered at a Greek restaurant near Strawberry to discuss their future, but due to the amount of ouzo consumed the only thing they could agree on was to compose a B-side on the spot.

Given its drunken genesis, 'Why Can't I Touch It?' boasts remarkably coherent and disciplined performances, particularly from John Maher and Steve Garvey. Maher's drumming is amongst the best of his career, and Garvey's steadfast bass riff provides a beautifully solid dance floor for

[120] Most oft-repeated by Steve Diggle.

[121] The instrumental 'Late For The Train' from *Love Bites*.

Shelley and Diggle's intertwined guitars to gambol upon. Lyrically Shelley was still attempting to find some substance in the emptiness of his soul, and failing, literally miserably.

The single was released on 29th March 1979 and made it to No. 29 in the charts. It was to be their last Top 30 single. Sensing the discord behind the songs, the band's designer Malcolm Garrett[122] produced a sleeve with a messy typeface and asymmetric angles. This was a sharp contrast to the neat and clear linear designs the band's previous singles and albums had been furnished with. As Shelley's next released song confirmed, something had gone badly wrong.[123]

Not that he or the rest of the band had time to work out exactly what. After recording demos for their next album the band were off on tour again. Visits to Europe, the UK and two trips to the USA were fitted around the recording and release of third album *A Different Kind Of Tension*. The emptiness and existential confusion that permeated the A- and B-sides of 'Everybody's Happy Nowadays' would go on to be the major theme of Shelley's songs on the album. 'I Don't Know What To Do With My Life' and 'Hollow Inside' make it clear from the titles alone, while the brilliant 'I Believe' ends the album's litany of confusion, with Shelley repeatedly screaming 'there is no love in this world anymore'.

By the end of the year Shelley was on the verge of a nervous breakdown and regularly threatened to leave the band. A long overdue break in live appearances was arranged

[122] Malcolm Garrett was a school (and Manchester Polytechnic) friend of Peter Saville, Factory's in-house designer. Garrett created Buzzcocks' iconic logo and his designs for Buzzcocks records (credited to 'Assorted iMaGes') were a significant part of their appeal, along with the bespoke badges that accompanied each release. I've still got mine.

[123] Shelley's appropriately titled 'Something's Gone Wrong Again' appeared on the B-side of 'Harmony In My Head', a song composed and sung by Diggle.

for the first half of 1980, though the band weren't entirely inactive. As well as continuing their various solo projects, by April they were in Pluto Studios demoing songs again. But though the layoff was just what Shelley needed, the band never recovered its momentum. Their final three singles,[124] largely recorded with Martin Hannett, weren't a great success, despite the band and producer's shared history. Hannett's production techniques, so wonderfully transformative when applied to Joy Division, were ill-suited to Buzzcocks. What's more, the man who had made emptiness an instrument in its own right, added keyboards and brass to a band who never needed anything more than guitars. Though he was only using new instrumentation to paper over the cracks, it was a demonstrably terrible idea.

Any chance of the three singles making the charts was further hampered by a steadfast refusal to pick A- and B-sides, with equal weight being given to Shelley and Diggle every time. Though this looked like a nice piece of egalitarianism, it only served to confuse the record-buying public. In any case Shelley's songs were not the bright pop of old, but dark and rather sinister. The darkest, 'Strange Thing', directly addressed his still growing depression. While Diggle's songwriting had clearly progressed since the last album, Hannett was largely unable to coax a decent vocal out of him and consequently mixed his voice frustratingly low. None of the singles made the charts, and the band split in early 1981 while attempting to record what would have been their fourth album at Pluto. Buzzcocks, the band who

[124] 'Part 1' featured Shelley's 'Are Everything' and Diggle's 'Why She's A Girl From The Chainstore'. 'Part 2' was 'Strange Thing' (Shelley) and 'Airwaves Dream' (Diggle). 'Part 3' was 'Running Free' and 'What Do You Know', which was mixed by Martin Rushent. Stripped of the ill-fitting brass parts, Shelley's 'What Do You Know' would have made a marvellous final single if it had been given precedence.

had done so much to transform the music scene of the late seventies, were no more. They were clearly never meant to be an eighties band.

Chapter 9
A Special Moment In Time

Joy Division
Unknown Pleasures

In April 1979, Factory Records booked Strawberry for three consecutive weekends in order to record the label's first LP. They had discovered a raw but thrilling Manchester post-punk band who had come together as a direct result of the Sex Pistols gig at the Lesser Free Trade Hall. They boasted an enigmatic lead singer whose profound lyrical depths were initially hidden to everyone, including the rest of the group. As much by luck as by good judgement, Factory paired the band with a maverick producer whose vision for their album was as fully realised – if equally enigmatic – as the lyricist's. Between them they created one of the most critically lauded albums ever. It was a record that had to be made in Manchester.

The circumstances that led to Joy Division recording their first album for Factory are, if anything, too well documented. Certainly the contract signing has become the stuff of legend, the story told in print and on celluloid many times over. Given the escalating amounts of blood involved, if they film it again Tony Wilson will have to lose an arm. Even so, it's difficult to overestimate the significance this signing had for what became *Unknown Pleasures*. If the band had signed to Martin Rushent's Genetic, which Rob Gretton was initially keen to do, they'd likely have recorded their first album with Rushent at Olympic in Richmond upon Thames. Rushent was a gifted producer who can count *Dare* by the Human League, *The Raven* by the Stranglers, as well as *Another Music In A Different Kitchen* by Buzzcocks amongst his many triumphs. Olympic was, and still is, an august venue with a huge sound, which has been responsible for many amazing records by numerous successful rock and pop acts from Adele to The Zutons by way of Prince, Queen and B.B. King. The resultant album would no doubt have been brilliant, but it most certainly would not have been *Unknown Pleasures*.

Luckily for posterity, Warner Bros, who held Genetic's purse strings, told Rushent to get his head out of his arse and sign someone like the Angelic Upstarts instead. Understandably peeved at being let down, Gretton, who never needed much persuasion as to the duplicitousness and unreliability of London folk anyway, immediately signed Joy Division to Factory – but only after Tony Wilson had guaranteed them the freedom to choose their own producer and artwork. They then set about arranging to record their first album, which they decided would be produced by Martin Hannett, and feature artwork by Peter Saville. Still, Joy Division's deal with Factory is oft-quoted as the best deal a band ever signed, mainly because it included the unprecedented arrangement whereby the label paid for the recordings but the band ended up owning them.

Martin Hannett was a bass player whose aptitude for mathematics and science inevitably coloured the way he approached recording. After he gained a chemistry degree from UMIST, he began his producing career with a couple of acts he'd seen round the Manchester folk clubs, namely the 'Belt & Braces Roadshow Band'[125] and Pete Farrow.[126]

---

[125] The Belt & Braces Roadshow Company was a socialist theatre company that produced a couple of heroically joyless and uncharismatic folk rock records on its own label in the early seventies. If they were the benchmark for acts on the Manc folk scene, it's no wonder Burke and Jerk went down a storm.

[126] He would later go on to produce Pete Farrow's mate, another notable stalwart of that scene, the inimitable John Cooper Clarke.

When he worked with Buzzcocks, he had no ambitions to alter anything. *Spiral Scratch,* he later stated, was 'a document. When you play it loud it sounds exactly as if you're right in front of the stage at one of their gigs.' After the EP was released he became the in-house producer for Tosh Ryan's Rabid Records, where he worked with Slaughter and The Dogs and on Jilted John's eponymous hit single. By the time he came to work on *Unknown Pleasures* with Joy Division, Hannett had already produced Orchestral Manoeuvres in the Dark[127] and A Certain Ratio for Factory, and had reached a significant conclusion: the erstwhile Martin Zero had decided he had zero interest in ever capturing a band's live sound again.

Joy Division's recording history up until *Unknown Pleasures* was patchy at best. Their first release was the self-produced *An Ideal for Living* EP,[128] recorded at Oldham's Pennine Studio. All four songs on the EP are strong, and the production stands up pretty well considering no one knew what they were doing. Unfortunately, though enthusiastic amateurism can often pay off in music recording, when it comes to manufacturing the actual record some degree of expertise is usually required. In this case the band's naivety shone through and would come back to haunt them in more ways than one. The recording deal they'd struck with Pennine included pressing 1,000 singles, without sleeves, which the band would provide themselves. This was a significant undertaking, paid for with a £600 bank loan for furniture that young married couple Ian and Debbie Curtis could ill-afford to pay back. So the

[127] The Hannett-produced version of OMD's 'Electricity' was never released. They went with the demo instead, though Hannett remixed it at Strawberry.

[128] They were called Warsaw when it was recorded, but Joy Division when it came out. Tracks were 'Warsaw', 'No Love Lost', 'Leaders Of Men' and 'Failures'.

band were justifiably horrified when they heard the finished product. While it's true to say that any pressing would struggle to cope with six minutes a side on a 7-inch, wherever Pennine were pressing their stuff was particularly ill-suited to the task. The record sounded like it was being played in a sack in the next room.

The other telltale sign of the band's distinct lack of foresight is the decision to go with Bernard 'Barney' Sumner's Hitler Youth-inspired sleeve design – he clearly had some fascination with Nazi imagery, which, while obviously being completely different to holding Nazi views, did leave the band wide-open to accusations of flirting with fascism. This wasn't helped by his decision to bill himself as the distinctly Germanic 'Bernard Albrecht' on the sleeve, possibly inspired by Albrecht Schönhals, star of Luchino Visconti's *The Damned* – the subject of which would seem to be right up Barney's strasse.[129] Also, on the roughly contemporaneous live compilation, *Short Circuit*, he can be heard berating the audience for not keeping still-imprisoned Deputy Führer Rudolph Hess in their thoughts.[130] Flirting? They were practically holding hands.

The band had also recorded demos for RCA, which they hated, and they had a track on the *Factory Sample* EP, 'Digital'. The revelatory sound of 'Digital' must have prompted their decision to engage Hannett to produce the album. It was recorded at Rochdale's 16-track Cargo Studios,[131] and

[129] Released in 1969, Visconti's *The Damned* depicts the rise of the Nazi party through its dealings with a wealthy industrial family.

[130] *An Ideal For Living*'s first song, 'Warsaw', is sung from Hess's viewpoint, and starts with his prison number.

[131] John Brierley's Cargo Studios' contribution to Manchester music is almost as legendary and pervasive as Strawberry's and Pluto's, and is as fully deserving of a book as they are. Maybe next time, eh?

appropriately enough Hannett used his signature AMS digital delay unit for the first time.[132] The results were so striking that both Factory and Joy Division thought Cargo was the perfect place to record the album, but Hannett had different ideas. The aspect of Joy Division which intrigued him the most was the space in their sound, which was most unusual at the time. While many producers would have looked to the natural ambience of the recording studio to showcase such fragile dynamics, Hannett was keen to find an environment with no dynamics at all, the better to provide his own. He also insisted that the album was recorded on 24-track. All of which meant there was only ever one candidate.

Strawberry had continued to go from strength to strength in the seventies. They had even been forced to take on a new apprentice engineer, Chris Nagle, to alleviate Peter Tattersall's frantic workload. Liverpool multi-arts collective The Scaffold recorded a couple of albums there, and the band's Mike McGear also cut a solo album with his brother producing – none other than Paul McCartney – thus fulfilling Eric Stewart's avowed ambition to get a Beatle across the threshold of the studio. Barclay James Harvest, Oldham's finest prog-rock band, made several albums there, as did Harvey Lisberg's new protégés Sad Café, whose breakthrough album *Facades* was produced by Eric Stewart. Of course, with hindsight their impact on Manchester's cultural landscape pales into relative insignificance compared to what was coming, but at least they paid the going rate. Tony Wilson's inheritance money aside, Factory was strapped for cash, but Peter Tattersall was good enough to cut them a deal. He agreed that Joy Division

[132] Advanced Music Systems was a Burnley-based company formed by aerospace engineers Mark Crabtree and Stuart Nevison. They invented the world's first digital delay unit, the AMS DMX 15-80, which Hannett used extensively. They were pioneers in digital recording and mixing and often used Hannett for beta testing.

could use the studio's 'downtime', i.e. overnight, with Chris Nagle engineering, at a much reduced fee. Nagle quickly earned his stripes and went on to work on most of the Factory recordings.

Thus *Unknown Pleasures* was recorded at Strawberry Studios. It was local enough to make Ian, Bernard, Peter and Steve feel at home and technologically advanced enough for Martin Hannett to feel the same. As such it was the only place in England capable of defining the Joy Division sound. Hannett took the material the band had hammered out in the North West's gob-filled shitholes and, without touching the arrangements, created an icy soundscape that will forever be intrinsically linked to Manchester.

While this transformation resulted in an album that counts among the best ever made, it's understandable that the members of Joy Division took a while to come to terms with its sonic landscape. After all, they had created a pretty good sound for themselves. Joy Division didn't need a producer to come in and tell them how they should sound, they already sounded brilliant. Everyone who saw Joy Division live, apart from Martin Hannett, knew that all the band needed to create a truly great album was a producer who could capture their live energy and Stooges-like power. I was lucky enough to witness their performance in a tiny youth club near Altrincham in March 1979, and they were very, very good, but by July when they played Belle Vue's The Mayflower[133] their set was like the end of the world. Steve Morris attacked his kit like it had done him an injustice and Hooky and Barney played like their life depended on it, their

[133] They appeared as part of a line-up that included The Fall, The Frantic Elevators, Ludus and The Distractions, amongst others. They were the best band by miles. The event was billed as 'Stuff The Superstars', a thinly-veiled dig at Buzzcocks and Magazine signing to major labels.

booming bass lines and searing melodies threatening to take the roof off. Maybe their lives did depend on it. But while they were merely brilliant, Ian Curtis was untouchable. It's worth noting that these were the days when it was almost a badge of honour to shuffle on in your day clothes and appear as 'normal' as possible, hence Mark E. Smith's working men's club-spiel and Pete Shelley's your-aunty-at-a-party persona. In this setting, Curtis's otherworldliness was so unexpected as to be almost disturbing. Has dancing ever looked so far divorced from having a good time? Was he in a trance, off his head on drugs or having some kind of seizure? Who knew? Not that it mattered anyway, it was like watching a shaman perform a ritual. And that voice! The perfect marriage of power and fragility, it could convey meaning even though you couldn't hear a word he said. It must have taken an exceptional vision, and one hell of an ego, to disregard the visceral power of Joy Division at their live peak and replace it with the delicate fragile sounds of *Unknown Pleasures*. Thankfully Hannett had plenty of both, and the marriage of Joy Division's songs and his vision was perfect. So perfect in fact that commentators are constantly in danger of elevating the personnel involved beyond the mere human, and human they demonstrably were.

It was Strawberry Studios that allowed Hannett to transcend the band's vision of themselves. He created a sound so different from contemporary rock that many, including the musicians who played it, initially struggled to appreciate what he'd done. Where Kraftwerk and Giorgio Moroder had previously created mechanical-sounding records by using synthesizers and analogue sequencers, Hannett had no such luxury. To produce the sound he had in his head he had to make three novice, untutored musicians sound as precise as machines. No mean feat, and he was really only able to pull it off thanks to 10cc. Eric Stewart was still obsessed with aping the close micing techniques of Steely Dan, and the band had continued to re-invest Strawberry's recording fees back into the studio in order to facilitate him. Strawberry now boasted walls lined with Colorado stone and clad in Californian pine, both of which absorbed sound in ways that even Abbey Road, still tiled in humble cork, couldn't manage. The resultant ambience-free sound greatly excited Hannett, as in his words it removed 'the clues the ear needs to recognise a room'. This gave him free rein to create an entirely new and entirely artificial room of his own, using synthesized echo, delay and reverb. Hannett had several go-to devices to achieve this effect,[134] some of which, notably those created by AMS, he has become synonymous with. Listening to Hannett describe this process on *Granada Reports*, the normally astute Mick Fleetwood commented 'Why not just use a real room?', which is akin to asking why Kraftwerk didn't just employ a real drummer. By creating an artificial space that was bigger than any real space could ever hope to be, Hannett 'gave each contributor all the room they needed – they were in their own zone, miles away from each other, and yet on top of each other' in the words of Paul Morley.

Hannett was in his element in Strawberry. Not content with recording the different musicians separately, to ensure no leakage between the sounds he hit on the idea of recording

[134] E.g. The Eventide Harmonizer and the Marshall Time Modulator. While in Strawberry he also used their 'Echo Plate', a pre-digital attempt at artificial ambience creation made by a German company called Elektro-Mess-Technik (EMT). It consisted of two huge wooden boxes containing pieces of sheet metal suspended from a steel frame and fitted with pickups. Transducers moved the sheet while the sound was played through it, creating the reverb effect. Weighing in at 600lbs plus, the presence of an EMT 140 was real evidence that a studio meant business.

the component parts of the drum kits separately too. Of course, playing those elements separately is completely unnatural and positively counter-intuitive for a drummer, so it's testament to Steve Morris's remarkable skill that the drums sound as fluent as they do.[135] This artificial disassembling of the drum patterns forced him into a distinctly robotic precision at times, and therein lies much of the magic of *Unknown Pleasures*.

As well as forcing Morris to ape the precise beats of a rhythm box, Hannett also manipulated the sound of his kit so that it resembled the synthesized sounds of a drum machine. Ironically, the reason those seventies drum machines sound so great is their complete inability, in those pre-sampling days, to sound like real drums. So you had real drums trying to sound like a machine poorly imitating real drums. And, as when the American bands copied The Beatles attempting to play like Americans, something new and rather wonderful ensued.

Hannett had several strategies to avoid interference from the people who had actually written and played what he saw as his impending masterpiece. He would insist that the air-conditioning was set to full blast in order to make the control room as inhospitable as possible. He would arrange last-minute mixing sessions in the witheringly early morning. When all else failed and Hooky and Barney turned up to try to get him to make the album sound like *them*, he had a standard instruction for Rob Gretton: 'Get these two thick stupid cunts out of my way.'

The album's opener, 'Disorder', starts with Steve Morris at his most industrial and mechanical, sounding for all the world like the beatbox on Cabaret Voltaire's near-simultaneous 'Nag

---

[135] It must have been a pain in the arse to record though, and Morris was reportedly reduced to tears on more than one occasion.

Nag Nag'. As on many of the tracks, the aggression of its live incarnation, which was usually played at breakneck speed, is replaced with something far more thoughtful. It could almost be described as 'dream-like' if that description didn't convey a sense of comfort, and there's nothing comforting about anything on *Unknown Pleasures*. When Ian asks 'Where will it end?' on the next track 'Day Of The Lords', the only thing you can be sure of is that it will be nowhere good. Once again, the drum sound is a revelation, and Hannett's keyboards lift the track considerably. He'd overdubbed these against the wishes of the musicians, without their knowledge. They didn't even hear them until the song was mixed.

It's a shame he didn't add keys to 'Candidate', which was written to order for the album, as it's pretty desperate for a lift from somewhere – Barney's guitar is so slight it's barely there. The lyric, like most of Curtis's best, blurs the boundaries between personal and universal. Is it political? Very possibly, but you're always left with that feeling that he's revealing something of himself, possibly too much. When he ends with 'I tried to get to you', it's amongst his most poignant lyrics.

'Insight' and 'She's Lost Control' both feature Steve Morris's pride and joy – his Synare 3 drum synthesiser. On 'Insight' it's set to the sound that most people associate with it – that slightly annoying 'Bo!' you hear on many seventies disco tracks, notably 'Love Don't Live Here Anymore' by Rose Royce. It sounds bizarrely out of context on 'Insight' though, and when he plays it on the instrumental break it sounds like a gun battle from *Star Wars*. On 'She's Lost Control' the Synare sounds more like sheet metal being struck.[136] Both songs showcase Morris at his most machine-like, in terms of

[136] Despite the fact that variations on those two sounds were pretty much all the Synare had to offer, it turns up on lots of late seventies records. Gary Numan and Ultravox were particularly enthusiastic proponents.

pattern and sound – 'She's Lost Control' in particular sounds unlike any other drum kit ever recorded.

Both of those songs also feature Hooky's trademark 'drone' bassline, where an open string (usually D) is played under the melody line.[137] This bass style, though unusual, was all the rage in Manchester at the time. It first appeared on 'Walking Distance', Steve Garvey's epic instrumental contribution to Buzzcocks' second album *Love Bites*, and can also be heard on The Fall's 'Underground Medecin' from *Live At The Witch Trials*. This rare bit of convergence from Manchester's original new wave only serves to underline just how different the three bands were.

The two best tracks on the album, 'Shadowplay' and 'New Dawn Fades', are unsurprisingly the quintessential Joy Division songs. A single repeated bass line and Bernard's beautifully expressive guitar work, one of the main features of which is his willingness to stop playing, are all that's required. The songs' dynamics are shockingly stark, and all the more atmospheric for it. 'Shadowplay' has the kind of dynamism that you only get from a song with a single riff – since you're only playing one thing, everything hinges on how you play it. And has there ever been a song where the music and lyric are so satisfyingly matched as 'New Dawn Fades'? It really is possible to 'admire the distance'.

'Interzone', the nearest the album gets to capturing their live sound – which isn't very near at all – features vocals by Pete Hook and was actually lifted from 'Keep On Keeping On' – a Northern soul classic by Nolan Porter.[138] They'd been persuaded to try and cover it when they were seeking

[137] He'd also go on to use it on his finest composition for Joy Division – 'Love Will Tear Us Apart'.

[138] A US-only single released in 1971.

a deal with RCA and copping the main riff was as near as they got.

'Wilderness' is probably the least personal lyric on the album, and has superficial similarities with 'Various Times' by The Fall,[139] as both songs' narrators travel through time and relate the atrocities they witness there. Mark E. Smith was the only Manchester lyricist at that time who could claim anything like parity with the Joy Division singer, though he was far less willing or able to tap into his emotions. Smith had genuine respect for Ian Curtis and was horrified when *Sounds* journalist Dave McCulloch used his lyrics ('that man died for you') in the magazine's ridiculously hagiographical reaction to Curtis's death.

It's true to say Curtis's lyrics are unremittingly unhappy and distracted throughout *Unknown Pleasures*, and portents of his eventual fate are there if you look for them.[140] 'I Remember Nothing' is particularly bleak, and when he declares 'I'm not afraid anymore' on 'Insight', you never quite believe him. But as with many fated artists, the benefit of hindsight solidifies what could be passing musings into direct statements of intent.[141] When the album was complete no one around the band was aware of the depths of Ian Curtis's despair, and it's entirely possible that that included Curtis himself. It's clear though that what sets Joy Division and *Unknown Pleasures* apart from the swathes of 'death' obsessed goth groups that

[139] The 'Ian' referred to in 'Various Times' is Ian McCulloch, not Curtis.

[140] 'It's creeping up slowly, That last fatal hour', 'Directionless, so plain to see, a loaded gun won't set you free, so you say', 'Dreams always end'.

[141] Once a band's fan base is rabid enough to pour over ever lyric some of them will see every word as a signifier. A sufficient percentage of The Beatles' audience was so obsessed with unearthing the facts about Paul McCartney's death from various lyrical clues that not even the obvious drawback that he was still alive could undermine their deductive reasoning.

followed in their wake was that the feelings expressed therein were palpably real, often uncomfortably so.[142] The fact that bands who thought that pale complexions and dark clothes equalled depth looked to Curtis for inspiration can hardly be laid at his door.

As Mick Middles puts it, Hannett's production for Joy Division 'shunted them forward five years'. Once the album was released, the parameters of Joy Division's sound were so intelligently set that it mattered less that *Closer* was committed to tape in London. By that stage the band and Hannett had a clear enough idea of what they wanted to say, and how they wanted to say it, so where they committed the songs to tape was more a question of logistics than aesthetics. But it's true to say that *Closer* doesn't quite equal its predecessor's simultaneously oppressive and expansive atmosphere. As every other factor was the same, much of the credit for that must go to Strawberry. Not least because Britannia Row's massive live room removed the need for artificial space, and thus gave Hannett less of a blank aural canvas on which to paint his pictures. Hannett made many more fine records, both for Factory and elsewhere, but he never reached such dizzying heights of production again. As with Curtis, his premature death robbed Manchester and the world of a prodigious talent.

The remaining members of Joy Division reconvened after the death of Ian Curtis with no clear idea of how to proceed. And Strawberry was the place where they were sufficiently at ease to begin the unenviable task of starting from scratch. Bernard Sumner, like Eric Stewart before him, was a guitarist with no ambition to be out front, who was

---

[142] Dreadful generalisation, I realise, but it explicitly refers to the bands. I'd never be so flippant as to dismiss the feelings of the listeners as unreal.

thrust into the spotlight when his band's singer departed. Both retreated to the womb of Strawberry Studios and tinkered with technology till they were ready to emerge, though neither ever completely embraced the role of frontman. And, with considerable help from their three associates of course, they went on to produce 'I'm Not In Love' and 'Blue Monday', two of the most innovative singles of the seventies and eighties respectively. And you couldn't play either of them live without help from machines.

Chapter 10
I Can't Find That Hole In The Wall

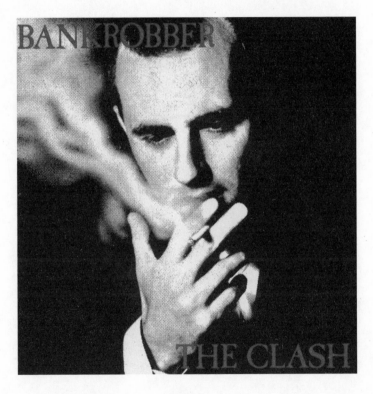

The Clash
Bankrobber

The Clash were an inspirational band, especially for would-be musicians. They were admirable for both their approachability and a greater level of industry than most of their contemporaries. From 1976 to May 1982, their level of output was remarkably prodigious. Comparison with John Lydon's productivity over the same period bears this out – Lydon produced less than 50 tracks, while The Clash recorded more than 120, all the while maintaining a frantic and relentless touring schedule.[143]

The Clash were such enthusiastic advocates of the time-honoured cycle of tour-rehearse-record they steadfastly neglected to factor in days off. Manchester in particular was always a place where The Clash struggled to sit still. They had a long-held affinity with the city: Collyhurst's Electric Circus was one of the few venues which honoured its booking on both the 'Anarchy In The UK' and 'White Riot' tours. They'd also been filmed for Granada TV at Belle Vue's Elizabethan Ballroom, and they played the Ardwick Apollo on 2nd July 1978 as part of the 'On Parole' tour. During this tour much of their downtime and soundchecks were taken up with filming scenes with Ray Gange for their celluloid 'masterpiece' *Rude Boy*. However, following the Apollo gig they found themselves with a day off. Buzzcocks' Steve Diggle

[143] The time it took for the Sex Pistols' break up and the formation of Public Image Ltd has to be taken into consideration, but that actually only took from January till May 1978. Breaking up one band and forming another seems to be the only thing Johnny Rotten ever did quickly in his life. Injury, injunction and indolence meant that after early 1977 Johnny appeared in public barely more often than Howard Hughes, and gigged only sporadically. Even the Pistols' much-discussed American tour was only seven dates long.

recalls that The Clash paid a visit to celebrated Manchester ale-house Tommy Ducks on this occasion, 'the one with the knickers on the ceiling' as Joe knew it.[144] While they were there they hastily arranged a secret gig at Rafters on Oxford Street for the same night.

The group presaged their punitive schedule for 1980 with shows on Christmas and Boxing Day 1979. These were staged at the Acklam Hall, a decidedly decrepit and ill-appointed North London community centre. The only way it evoked the spirit of Christmas was the way it huddled under the West Way like a Dickensian match-girl sheltering from the snow. Their mythically impecunious lifestyle notwithstanding, the band's homes must have been truly atrocious if that was the best place they could find to see out the holidays. The band didn't really owe the audience a great show – after all they must have had nowhere better to go either – but by all accounts The Clash put even more effort into these impromptu gigs than they did their normal shows. They gave two marvellously upbeat performances which incorporated songs that they never performed elsewhere, notably 'Keys To Your Heart' by Joe's previous outfit The 101'ers. The second gig also included a tentative run through of an as-yet-unrecorded track they had been working on in soundchecks. It was a ska number which told the unusual tale of a bank thief with an aversion to violence. They followed up these Acklam Hall gigs with a slot at the Hammersmith Odeon as part of the 'Concert For Kampuchea', where the nascent 'Bankrobber' was aired once

[144] In the 1990s, the much-loved Tommy Ducks found itself in the way of corporate-backed urban renewal. When its temporary preservation order ran out on 12th February 1993, brewers Greenall had it demolished overnight before a new order could be placed. They gladly paid the £150,000 they were fined, a figure dwarfed by the amount they got for the land. Depressingly, the site where a unique Manchester landmark once stood now houses a Premier Inn, a Total Fitness and a Costa. That's progress.

again. This was a filmed benefit spread over four days and featured Wings, The Who, Ian Dury and The Specials, among others. By all accounts Mick joining the Blockheads on stage that night didn't sit well with Joe. 'We are The Clash,' Joe told him. '*We* – not four *Is*.' He clearly thought all Mick's energies should be saved for band business, as his always were.

February 3rd and 4th of 1980 saw The Clash take to the stage at the Manchester Apollo again, as part of their '16 Tons' tour, which had begun on 5th January. After that they had a little free time, but not enough to go home, so their incessant desire to keep the motor running led them to invest in some studio time in the city. As the group were used to a fairly high recording standard by now, this inevitably meant Pluto Studios, the only state-of the-art recording facility situated in Manchester city centre. Following its move from Stockport, Pluto was now housed just down from the Old Garratt pub on Granby Row. The Garratt was a classic Boddingtons pub which drew a younger than average clientele. It served as the staging area for several clubs in the area, including The Cyprus Tavern and 42nd Street. In both of these clubs, and indeed on the jukebox of the Garratt itself, you were never more than 10 minutes away from a Clash song, so the band were clearly on friendly soil.[145]

It's a mark of just how strong the work ethic was in The Clash that their first impulse on gazing at the empty calendar was to book a recording session for that frosty February evening. There was certainly no pressure on them from

[145] The Old Garratt, like many popular Manchester ale houses, was subjected to a thorough renovation in the 1990s, though not as thorough as Tommy Ducks. As well as the inevitable elimination of the jukebox, this 'improvement' saw the removal of all upholstery and carpets, to the point where the most comfortable place to sit was the toilets.

Columbia/CBS.[146] The Clash's record label were happy to follow-up their previous single 'London Calling' with another track from the remarkable album of the same name; both preceding Clash albums had yielded two singles, and *London Calling* had only been released the previous December. The Clash had different ideas. Two years earlier, when CBS had lifted the mediocre 'Remote Control' as a single from their debut album behind their backs, the band were so annoyed they stuck it to the man by writing and recording the infinitely catchier 'Complete Control'.[147] This time they were determined to avoid another album track being forced down the single-buying public's throat.

They resolved to draw an unbreachable line under their previously released material. With no little amount of hubris they decided they would record and issue a brand-new 45 every month for the next year. Without stopping for a moment to ask the opinion of anyone at CBS, and to ensure common sense didn't have the chance to get the better of them, they got down to business. This is a fantastic example of just how much times have changed: it's unthinkable that any artist today would actively and openly attempt to frustrate their record company's efforts to maximise profits. The Clash seem to have made a career of it. They insisted that their double and triple albums were sold for the price of a single LP, knowing full well that they were reducing their own incomes too. Naively or not, they also repeatedly snuck non-paying punters into their shows and boasted of the fact in song. They often insisted on reduced ticket prices too.

Mikey Dread, support act for the 16 Tons tour, was chosen to act as producer and co-arranger at the session, presumably for

---

[146] At this time Columbia was forced to call itself 'CBS' in the UK to avoid confusion with EMI's Columbia.

[147] 'They said release "Remote Control", but we didn't want it on the label.'

reasons of proximity as much as anything else. He had joined the tour in Scotland a couple of weeks previously, straight from Jamaica, the first time he had ever seen snow. Born Michael Campbell in 1954, Mikey was a DJ, label owner, composer and performer. He was also an experienced record producer who'd worked with Lee 'Scratch' Perry and Sugar Minott. The Clash had been introduced to his work by Don Letts and engaged him as support for the lion's share of the tour. They'd always strived to get interesting and unusual support acts, whether the audience appreciated it or not, and they often didn't. Grandmaster Flash got a particularly difficult ride.

The entrance to Pluto was so anonymous that when The Fall recorded *Perverted By Language* there a couple of years later, it took me half an hour to find it, despite the fact I'd spent most Saturday nights for the last two years in the Old Garratt. One can only hope The Clash had less trouble. Once inside the heavily-fortified door however, they would have felt right at home. The polished wood, smoked glass and mood lighting all contributed to the workmanlike ambience, and whatever the time of day, in the studio it felt like late evening.

They decided to record the ska number they'd performed at Acklam Hall and the Odeon at the tail end of the previous year. However, something in the atmosphere moved the band to transform it from a dance number to something far weightier; a stately reggae folk song. Though Topper Headon was a dab hand at ska and reggae, the drums on 'Bankrobber' are stylistically more akin to 'New Dawn Fades' or 'I Remember Nothing' from Joy Division's *Unknown Pleasures*, released in June of the previous year. Whether subconscious or deliberate (the geography could have brought them to mind), the appropriation of Steve Morris's melancholy shuffle gives the song an aura of Mancunian sadness that's notably absent from all other Clash singles. It's the same tangible sadness that haunted the material Neil Sedaka recorded at Strawberry eight years previously.

From the moment the booming bass riff kicks in, following a heavily-reverbed snare intro, it's clear that 'Bankrobber' is the most pared-down single The Clash ever released. In terms of melody, that bass line, which is unchanged throughout, carries the whole thing. Mick Jones's guitar has never been so anonymous, acting more like a percussion instrument throughout the song. In fact, apart from providing a wobbly synth line towards the end, and some of the sound effects, Mick takes something of a back seat all round here. Even the backing vocals, usually his forte, are provided by Mikey. Mikey wasn't averse to the odd sound effect himself. He had a stock of what their road manager, Johnny Green, called 'farmyard noise toys from a joke shop', which he'd previously used to keep bass player Paul Simonon amused on the tour bus.[148] The producer would use anything that came to hand to achieve the correct vibe, including matchboxes and squeaky rubber animals.

Joe's warm and personable vocal performance on 'Bankrobber' counts among his best. That said, it had to be to carry off the somewhat silly words, which certainly attracted some criticism on the single's release. The *Sounds* review in particular took umbrage at Joe's claims about his father's chosen profession, pointing out that Mr Mellor senior was in fact a middle-ranking secretary at the Foreign Office. This is clearly a specious argument as few would argue that 'Moonage Daydream' is a failure because David Bowie was not really an alligator. But

[148] Johnny Green was the stage manager, chief roadie, driver, minder and babysitter for The Clash from 1977 to 1982. He was a thoroughly unreasonable voice of reason and his book *A Riot of Our Own* captures the madness of recording and touring with The Clash perfectly. His interactions with Ray Gange are also the highlights of the film *Rude Boy*, along with the brilliant live footage.

it's a shame that such a hauntingly crepuscular aural hybrid was accompanied by a slight, and slightly preposterous, lyric.

Joe had flirted with the concept of rock star as outlaw before, when he chose to record Sonny Curtis's 'I Fought The Law', and would again on Eddy Grant's 'Police On My Back'. But the lyric of 'Bankrobber' is at least sufficiently self-aware to point out that the narrator isn't man enough to follow in his father's footsteps. He's far too busy getting his hair right. And while altogether too upbeat for its musical setting, it does make for a great singalong.[149]

To the surprise of no one, The Clash's one-year-plan never did come to fruition. Maurice Oberstein, the head of CBS, took one listen to 'Bankrobber' and refused to release it. According to The Clash, he declared it sounded like 'all David Bowie's records played backwards at once' which was a bizarre statement in a number of ways. For one, it's patently obvious that it doesn't, and for another, as Tony Fletcher pointed out in *The Clash – A Complete Guide To Their Music*, 'Why would that not be of interest?' It's likely Oberstein took this stance in an attempt to force the band into releasing a second single from *London Calling*. The Clash, to their credit, refused to play ball. They snuck 'Bankrobber' out in Holland and waited till the import sold so many copies that CBS were forced to release it in the UK. It subsequently became one of their biggest singles and the nation was treated to the peculiar spectacle of Legs and Co dancing to it on *Top of the Pops*. The whole episode cemented The Clash's us-and-them attitude to the record company so securely that Strummer was still mildly miffed when discussing the matter with Don Letts in *Westway To The World* a full twenty years later.

[149] Mikey Dread's vocal on the B-side is sung over the same backing track and it's even more unbecomingly jovial than 'Bankrobber'. At one point he even relates how he shrugged off the harsh Scottish winter with a nice hot bath. ('You jump into the tub and then you sud and then you sud.') Lovely.

While they disregarded the essentially disposable lyrical themes of the single's A- and B-sides, the potential of the aural marriage of reggae and haunted Manchester post-punk created by The Clash on that wet February night was not lost on the next generation of British musicians. A year later, The Specials, who'd played with The Clash on the night of one of the song's earliest outings, took the seriously indebted 'Ghost Town' to the top of the charts. They'd furnished it with a lyric that was infinitely more downhearted than 'Bankrobber' which matched the mood of its musical landscape flawlessly. It provided the perfect soundtrack to the troubled times, as Manchester burned in the light of the Moss Side riots.

*

Someone who was present when 'Bankrobber' was recorded eventually used this Clash-in-Manchester attitude and sonic template to inform one of the biggest bands the area ever produced. Due to The Clash's lack of choice when it came to booking a studio, über fans Ian Brown and Pete Garner were able to meet up with their heroes despite having no real clue of the band's plans. Vaguely aware that The Clash were up to something in Manchester, Ian and Pete bunked the train from Timperley and set out to track down the band, just as Graham Nash and Allan Clark had pursued The Everly Brothers to their hotel twenty years before.

'Pluto was the only studio we knew in town,' Garner said later, 'so we sat on the wall opposite in the rain.'

After several minutes listening to nothing but the raindrops beating out a rhythm on the roof of the Old Garratt's porch, the sound of Topper Headon's drums floated out into the misty Manchester night and confirmed they were in the right place. With that, as Ian recalled, 'We knocked on the door, they let us in and we hung round for a bit.' The Clash definitely were an unusual band, it seems. In return for nothing more than helping the band locate a fast food outlet, the two young men were given access all areas. Ian recalls Joe spending several minutes clicking his fingers in time with the studio's grandfather clock. Though he took a number of lessons about being in a band from that night, alas for Geffen, he never learned to check the studio clock himself.

Even before being allowed such unfettered access to the band, Ian was convinced of their almost preternatural power, and this faith in their potential for restitution was responsible for one of his life's pivotal moments. In 1977, on an otherwise unremarkable day at Altrincham Grammar, he'd seen someone getting beaten up and thought 'that's that kid who lives up our road'. As he explained to *The Guardian* in 2010: 'I pulled the other kid off because he'd had enough, then I went round that night to see if he was all right, and I took the first Clash album… He went and bought it the next day, and played it every day for about 18 months, before and after school. That got him obsessed with guitar and made him want to play.' John Squire never looked back.

Ian Brown has always used The Clash as the yardstick for measuring a band's greatness, and he never thought The Stone Roses measured up to his idols. 'I have arguments with people who say we were better than the Pistols or The Clash,' he explained in 1994. 'To me, we never touched [them].'

Years later, another cold winter's night in Manchester saw the singer reunite with his boyhood heroes. On 2nd December 2011, at a benefit concert for the Hillsborough Justice Campaign, Ian and John, newly reunited themselves, were joined on stage by Mick Jones. They played the tune that Ian had first heard wafting above the Manchester skyline some 31 years before. It seems 'Bankrobber' will always be a Manchester song.

Clearly it was happenstance that brought The Clash to Pluto recording studio in February 1980. They were in Manchester, and their inability to exist as people unless they were functioning as a band meant that was where they would record. They probably had no conscious desire to emulate the vibe of the post-punk Manchester bands that were nipping at the heels of the class of '77. However, it's telling that the product of their time in Pluto was sonically more akin to the epic soundscapes of 'New Dawn Fades' by Joy Division or 'Music Scene' by The Fall than the cranked up rock and roll of 'Clash City Rockers'. Even the hugely inventive 'London Calling', which ingeniously evoked the post-apocalyptic landscape of Joe's lyrics in its music, was structured fairly traditionally.

'Bankrobber', on the other hand, was the first Clash single that wasn't really a song at all. Like the aforementioned Manchester bands – and Public Image Ltd on their inspired and inspiring second album *Metal Box* – The Clash created a soundscape and let the structure work itself out. In The Clash's case, they used reggae as a template, rather than the Krautrock favoured by The Fall and PiL, but 'Bankrobber' wasn't lovers rock, it was a bass riff and a wobbly melody line sung by someone with more passion than technical ability. The spirit of Manchester music writ large.[150]

---

[150] Suitably inspired by the idea of soaking up the local vibe while recording, The Clash began work on their next album in New York the very next month. The ambience of the Big Apple informed much of *Sandinista*; the sound and lyrics of 'The Magnificent Seven', 'Lightning Strikes' and 'Broadway' are all directly attributable to the band's prolonged stay.

Chapter 11
It Takes Grace To Play The Second Fiddle Well

The Fall
Perverted By Language

While it's true that The Fall recorded *Dragnet* and *Grotesque* at Cargo Studios, it's curious that many of the group's early records, including their first, were recorded well away from Greater Manchester. Even *Slates*, the 10-inch mini album which featured 'Leave The Capitol', was recorded in London. As 'Leave The Capitol' was Smith's 'definitive rant' against all aspects of London living, this was probably deliberate. Perhaps he couldn't summon sufficient bile to power his performance anywhere else.[151]

Joy Division and The Smiths recorded their first albums near home, and both records are tinged with, and benefit from, a palpable air of Mancunian melancholy. But if one thing's clear about Mark E. Smith, it's that he would never allow such territorial sentimentality to inform his decisions. Perhaps more than any other 'post-punk' artist, Smith has been defined by his connection to Manchester and Salford, as much as he attempts to deny it. Maybe that's why The Fall can record anywhere. Everywhere they go, they always take the Manchester weather with them.

Mark E. Smith also often attempts to downplay the significance of witnessing the Sex Pistols at the Lesser Free Trade Hall. But that was the event that convinced him that the vague poetry readings and loose jams he and his friends indulged in after the pub could be turned into a fully functioning band. It's possible it may not even have been his idea. The first proper line-up of The Fall, featuring Tony Friel on bass, Una Baines

[151] This disconnected conjecture isn't an affectation, by the way. I had no input whatsoever into where the band recorded, and I wasn't afforded much insight into Mark's decision-making process either.

on keyboards, Martin Bramah on guitar and Karl Burns on drums, was a much more democratic organisation than we usually think of when considering the group. Lyrics weren't even the sole province of the singer; 'Dresden Dolls', written by Una, was one of the highlights of their early live set until her departure rendered it out of bounds. An absolutely brilliant live band by all accounts, this fondly-remembered line-up never made it past their first EP, *Bingo-Master's Break-Out!*[152] In fact it was consigned to history well before the record was even released. By the time The Fall came to record their second single 'It's The New Thing', Una and Tony Friel were gone, to be replaced by Yvonne Pawlett and Marc Riley respectively. This was the line-up that recorded The Fall's first album *Live At The Witch Trials*, and the first iteration of The Fall I ever saw live.[153] They should, and very possibly even could, have been massive. Besides their obviously unique vocalist, they boasted a genuinely innovative guitar hero and one of the most inventive drummers Manchester ever threw up. Sadly, Karl was only too aware of how good he was and soon sought out a bigger stage.[154] His replacement by Mike Leigh had a profound effect on the group's sound – it's hard to imagine two drumming styles (or personalities for that matter) more at odds. In fact it's probable that the main reason for Mike's recruitment was his utter dissimilarity to Karl.

[152] The recording of the EP, which consisted of the title track plus 'Psycho Mafia' and 'Repetition', was paid for by Buzzcocks and initially slated for release on New Hormones. They didn't have the money, so the tapes were passed to Miles Copeland and Mark Perry's Step Forward label.

[153] At The Apollo in Manchester 19th August 1978, supporting The Rezillos. For years I was convinced that the first time I saw them was at Kelly's, with The Distractions, but while writing this book I discovered that wasn't till the October. That research wasn't all for nothing, then.

[154] He briefly played with Public Image Ltd, though nothing was ever commercially released. By all accounts they got on like a house on fire.

But it was the subsequent loss of Mark E. Smith's main songwriting partner, Martin Bramah, which affected him, and thus The Fall, the most. Possibly more than the loss of any other member before or since. 'I shit myself,' Smith told the BBC years later.[155] Losing such a key member was clearly a painful process, and at that point he determined that no one person would have such a pivotal role in The Fall again. He didn't succeed, but it wasn't for lack of trying on his part.

Against the odds, Bramah's departure from the group was more than ably covered by the addition of Craig Scanlon and Steve Hanley on guitar and bass, with Riley moving to second guitar.[156] This line-up remained pretty much the same for the next three years, give or take the odd drummer. They recorded only one album with Mike Leigh, the brilliant, if bewildering, *Dragnet*. It was a significant reboot as, apart from Smith, everyone was new to their position. The album's production was purposely unsettling and opinion on its merits amongst Fall fans is highly polarised.[157] It amplified the album's differences from its predecessor to such a ridiculous degree that *Live At The Witch Trials* and *Dragnet* barely sound like the same group. They weren't, really.

The musicians that recorded The Fall's third album, *Grotesque*, comprised of three school friends and a younger brother.[158] As such, this line-up was the first that was potentially more loyal to each other than to Smith. He eventually addressed

[155] He added 'Not literally', in case you were wondering.

[156] Once Yvonne jumped ship Marc alternated between guitar and keyboards.

[157] I think it sounds terrible, but there you go.

[158] It's at this point I briefly enter the story. For obvious reasons, I was reluctant to include an album I was on in a history of significant Manchester recordings. But I was editorially persuaded that there was a Fall-shaped hole in the narrative, and while I could have written about the band's time at Strawberry (which I wasn't involved in) it seemed a bit perverse, if you'll pardon the pun. I'll try not to be a distraction.

this imbalance by re-introducing Karl Burns into the mix, initially as a stand-in drummer when American immigration said I was too young to play American clubs.[159] The tour was a great success, Karl was as brilliant as ever, and everyone enjoyed having him around. The Fall subsequently took a trip to Iceland with me back behind the kit but on our return Karl came on board permanently and the two-drummer line-up was born.

The next album featured two tracks recorded in Iceland[160] with the rest recorded at The Regal, a converted cinema in Hitchin, Hertfordshire. *Hex Enduction Hour* was 60 minutes of intense and esoteric polemic, set against the band's thorniest set of backing tracks to date. Almost despite itself, it was also something of an artistic peak. Much to the band's astonishment, it garnered both critical approbation and fairly decent sales. This was despite it being released on Kamera Records, a mainly heavy metal label whose most famous recording artist was Freddie Starr. The unexpected interest panicked Smith a little, and sure enough the band's next release confounded the critics and record-buying public alike, and thus scuppered any upward momentum. Whether this was a conscious decision on Mark Smith's part remains conjecture, even to those of us who were there. Smith himself has both confirmed and denied it in interviews, depending on whatever particular point he had to make that day.

The resultant seven-track EP, *Room To Live*, was a fairly dismal collection of half-finished songs, most of which

[159] This was the official line, at least. Didn't seem to be an issue the next time we went, despite the fact I was still only 19. Probably Mark thought such a gruelling schedule was too much to ask of a just-17-year-old. He may well have been correct.

[160] Having successfully recorded 'Hip Priest' (possibly the band's most popular song) and 'Look, Know' (slated for the next single) Mark declared 'Right! We've wasted enough time!' and got the band to compose and record 'Iceland' on the spot. We were only in there a day. As gestation periods go, it's hardly *The Second Coming*, is it?

featured only a fraction of the band. A fair percentage of it amounts to self-sabotage, particularly on 'Marquis Cha-Cha'. Boasting one of Smith's funniest, most sinister lyrics, in which he casts himself as a Lord Haw-Haw for the Falklands War, the song was treated to a slipshod, under-rehearsed backing with glaring errors and wonky timekeeping. Even worse, the album's final track, 'Papal Visit', only features Mark (on violin!) and Karl.[161]

The band then set off on a gruellingly extensive Australasian tour. As ever with long tours, interpersonal relationships were pushed to breaking point just as live performances were honed to new heights of cohesiveness. The tracks that were recorded for *Room To Live* were particularly transformed, having been properly learnt and arranged over the course of the tour. Shortly after we got back, Smith seized the opportunity to rid the band of both an unwanted air of professionalism and an unwanted voice of dissent by sacking Marc Riley.

It's often convincingly argued that this periodic pressing of the reset button is what has allowed The Fall to constantly exist for forty-plus years, but like many frontmen and women whose every utterance is given a forum, Smith is apt to rewrite history to make everything look planned. The truth was he couldn't stand Marc Riley by this stage and the feeling was pretty much mutual. If getting rid of the band's guitarist and keyboard player necessitated a move to a sparser and more hollowed out musical landscape, then of course that would be the sound he'd wanted all along.

The Fall's entourage was further slimmed down when Kay Carroll, the band's long-term manager and Mark's partner, finally snapped midway through the subsequent US tour.

[161] I'd love to give you my opinion on this brave and innovative subversion of the entire rock genre, but I've never heard it. I probably should have, as research for this book if nothing else, but I took a vow at the time. I'm sure you understand.

Following a not untypical bar room infraction she refused to carry on. She never returned home, not even to move out of the flat she shared with Mark. She'd clearly had enough.

The group's next single, 'The Man Whose Head Expanded', released in July 1983, was the first recorded example of this new regime, with Riley's nagging keyboard riff remaining defiantly unreplaced.[162] It was recorded in London, in a tiny studio with insufficient room for two drum kits, which may well explain why Karl played second bass on both 'The Man Whose Head Expanded' and its B-side, 'Ludd-Gang'.[163]

As well received as *Hex Enduction Hour* was, one of the reasons it sounded so dense was that Regal's 16-track desk had struggled to cope with two full drum kits, so for the next album it was decided that we would record on 24-track. Seeking to keep costs to a minimum,[164] Mark decided that we should also record at home in Manchester. Now that the band was back on Rough Trade, it fell to label boss Geoff Travis to find a suitable studio, and he contacted Pluto. Aware of Keith Hopwood's willingness to use the studio's commercial sector profits to subsidise new music, and despite his image as a genial and business-averse hippy, Travis negotiated a heavily-discounted rate.

By the time The Fall found their way to Granby Row,

[162] The riff went on to form the basis of Marc Riley & The Creepers' 'Jumper Clown'. If proof were ever needed that Mark E. Smith's frequent assertion that 'Riley wanted to be in a pop band' was nonsense, then 'Jumper Clown' is it. It makes 'The Man Whose Head Expanded' sound like Steps.

[163] Or maybe not. When we recorded 'Lie Dream Of A Casino Soul', which featured my (rather catchy, I thought) drum riff, Mark insisted that Karl played it. When re-recording the next single 'Look, Know' (the Iceland version wasn't used), for which Karl had written a brilliant drum part, Smith had me play it. ~~The awkward twat.~~ A brilliant piece of conceptual wrong-footing.

[164] Following Kay's acrimonious departure, Mark's hands were now firmly on the band's purse strings. Which is probably the reason me, Steve, Heather (Steve's wife), Craig, Karl and Sol the driver nearly starved to death in Germany. Good times.

Pluto was ticking along quite nicely. Phil Bush, the chief engineer, was working 18 hours a day, and Keith Hopwood was now writing jingles for TV and radio commercials, as well as recording them. Typically the studio would be used for jingles three or four days in the week and the rest of the time would be taken up with bands. Like its 'big brother' Strawberry, Pluto featured an acoustically dead recording room, though it also featured a 'live' area, usually used for recording drums. Keith Hopwood had used his advertising revenue to kit the studio out with a prestigious Trident Series 80 console and a Studer A800 24-track recorder. The studio's decor was still fairly seventies looking though, with every surface clad in noise reducing brown baize. In fact the wall covering was so pervasive it even made it into the lyric of 'Garden'.

Under the auspices of producer Steve Parker, The Fall entered Pluto's relatively upmarket city-centre recording facility to record its sparsest album to date, for the most part shorn of both rhythm guitar and keyboards. Just as The Clash had done in the same room two years earlier, the band set about replacing their customary wall of sound with something altogether more ethereal.

Craig Scanlon rose to the challenge of complete responsibility for melody with considerable aplomb. The album's twin high points, 'Smile' and 'Garden', really highlighted his ability for unexpected yet entirely appropriate harmony. Pluto's bespoke 24-track soundscape gave his guitar real room to breathe. The studio was ideally suited to the two drum-kit line-up too, thus *Perverted By Language* was the first time the contrast between the two disparate drumming styles was crystal clear. The bass sound was a little disappointing at times, which is probably the reason a live version of 'Tempo House' from the

Haçienda was used on the final album, as the bass line was most of the song.[165] It had so many words that onstage it often lasted twelve minutes or more, but the version that made the album (recorded at the Haçienda on 27th July) clocked in at a relatively brusque 8:52.

Mark Smith wasn't happy with Pluto's more expansive sound at all. 'Rough Trade put us in some crap studio for four days,' he later commented.[166] It's doubtful he was aware of Pluto's link to Manchester's musical heritage, and even more doubtful he'd have been impressed, though he did once admit to a grudging liking for Peter Noone when he was 14.

Smith responded to the simpler musical palette by delivering his most oblique set of lyrics to date. While the broadly autobiographical bits of 'Eat Y'self Fitter' were self-explanatory[167] (Kellogg's-referencing chorus apart) most lyrics offered no such clarity. Was 'Garden' a treatise on the nature of man's relationship with God since expulsion from Eden, a sideways look at the dank underbelly of suburbia, or both? Possibly, but then Mark wasn't telling. He certainly wasn't telling me.

Elsewhere 'Smile' featured a semi-affectionate pen portrait

[165] The recording was taken from video. Though we'd encountered it before, at Minneapolis' First Avenue earlier in the year, the Haçienda was an early UK pioneer of simultaneous video screening at gigs. The videos were also recorded with the sound taken from the desk. Lots of these videos were later released commercially by Factory. Anyone watching should bear in mind that the crystal clear audio bears no relation to what was actually heard on the night. The sound in the Haçienda was abysmal.

[166] Not that such withering criticism should be a cause of concern for Keith Hopwood – Smith famously mastered *Bend Sinister* from a C90 cassette because he preferred its sound to John Leckie's lovingly wrought final production. They never worked together again.

[167] The 'met a hero of mine' verse tells the tale of when Mark met John Cale after the latter's gig at the Haçienda on 10th March 1983. Legend has it that Cale's set was so quiet, Pete Hook and Marc Riley had to walk through the crowd telling them to stop talking.

of Karl Burn's indiscreet personality and dress sense – 'Would ask for a fag in Texas' could go on his gravestone. 'I Feel Voxish' offered the pointedly sinister 'I've been sharpening a knife in the bathroom, on a brick I got from the garden. No one will fuck with me again.' Definitely not the Garden of Eden that time.

Of course, it would be remiss of me to offer critique or praise to tracks I was so closely involved in, but clearly the words had nowt to do with me. As Mr Smith so generously put it when commenting on the role of the other members of The Fall in 'Hexen Definitive/Strife Knot': 'You know nothing about it. It's not your domain. Don't confuse yourself with someone who has something to say.'

Perish the thought.

Midway through making the album it became clear to everyone in the band that things were about to change. Brix, Mark's new girlfriend, who he'd met on tour in the US, had been a constant presence throughout the subsequent tours of Europe and the UK. She was very quiet at first, but she was willing to help out and ended up doing the lights most nights. Mark was clearly besotted with her and, more importantly for the rest of us, she had a distinctly positive effect on his mood and manners. So when he announced that we were going to record a song with Brix playing guitar and singing[168] no one was massively surprised or offended. To be honest, it was his intention to get his violin out again that worried us most. 'Hotel Bloedel' was completely different from the rest of the album, but everyone did their best on it. And it did sound like The Fall, just not much like any Fall that had gone before, and it never made it into the live set. When the band toured in the autumn, Brix first took

[168] He deliberately didn't mention that she'd written the whole thing.

to the stage to sing and play guitar on 'C.R.E.E.P', the next song to be written.

The album came with an accompanying video, though the tracks don't really match. Factory had created a video offshoot, 'Factory Ikon', initially to capture the live performances at the Haçienda, but in-house 'VJ' Claude Bessy and director Malcolm Whitehead had loftier ambitions. Not much loftier ambitions, it has to be said, as you'll know if you've ever seen *Perverted By Language Bis*, but somehow they persuaded Rough Trade to reluctantly stump up some cash for a long form video. Clips were filmed for 'Eat Y'self Fitter', 'Wings' and 'Kicker Conspiracy', including footage shot in Pluto.[169] The resultant VHS release was bulked out with live clips, including the video of 'Tempo House' which also made the album. Mark accurately likened the distinctly amateurish production values to *Granada Reports'* outside broadcasts ('tea-time TV'). If nothing else, they were a much-needed way of highlighting his keen sense of humour, which though present in many of his lyrics wasn't always immediately obvious. They're also a matchless document of the band's ability to laugh at itself.

Given the direction The Fall went off in next, *Perverted By Language* stands alone. Though the idea that Brix took the band in a completely new direction and turned The Fall into a shiny pop band has been somewhat exaggerated, it's clear that the band's next phase was a departure. Album centrepiece 'Tempo House' left the set by the end of the year and was never played live again. Between the stresses of the Australian tour, Marc Riley's sacking and Kay Carroll's ignominious departure in the US, the band's mood had been in something

[169] If you watch the clips from Pluto you can see that Craig didn't get the message that we were to be videoed. That's definitely a bottom-of-the-ironing-pile 'Souvenir from Greece' t-shirt he's wearing.

of a downward spiral since *Room To Live*. It was time for a change, and Brix's arrival provided just the catalyst. The sparse and doleful Mancunian mood of *Perverted By Language* wasn't going to be revisited anytime soon.

Chapter 12
So Much To Answer For

The Smiths
The Smiths

The Smiths are the apex of Manchester bands in many ways, representing the perfect fulcrum between the individualist angst of the post-punk bands and the sunny inclusiveness of Madchester and Oasis. What's more, in Johnny Marr they could boast a composer whose skill and dedication to his craft harked back to the classic songwriters of the sixties.

It's entirely fitting that they recorded their debut single at Strawberry and their first album at Pluto. From day one Morrissey and Marr, as avid students of music and musical mythology, had one eye on creating the perfect mythos around the band. Even their first meeting was carefully choreographed by Marr to echo the original assignation between Jerry Lieber and Mike Stoller,[170] so it's tempting to believe that they were fated to record their first records at Manchester's two iconic studios. What's more, despite his protestations that Manchester meant 'nothing' to him, Morrissey always had a keen interest in the city's folklore and was also a particular fan of Herman's Hermits, who he 'devoured' according to Johnny Marr. As well as his wonderful version of 'East West', he later admitted he'd 'blushed for a fortnight' when Peter Noone name-checked him on his US TV show, so he must have been massively pleased at Pluto's direct link to the band.

From the very beginning, The Smiths' career path was like something from a movie: the rise to fame of The Little Ladies from *Rock Follies* was scarcely more far-fetched. Their first gig

[170] The legendary US songwriters of 'Hound Dog', 'Stand By Me' and hundreds of others.

was at Manchester's Ritz, albeit as support, and by their fifth they were attracting big enough audiences to headline their own London show. There's no doubt at all that their brilliance and utter uniqueness fully justified such a meteoric ascent, but it does make you wonder what exactly Morrissey has had to moan about over the years. He literally gained a lifelong, artistically uncompromised and fantastically remunerative profession without leaving the house. After all, Johnny Marr was not only the most talented guitarist of his generation, he also brought Joe Moss along, a friendly and passionate manager who was endlessly supportive, both personally and financially. Unsurprisingly, as people do when they get things too easily, Morrissey took them both for granted.[171]

'Hand In Glove', The Smiths' first single, was recorded at Strawberry Studios on Sunday 27th February 1983. The Smiths were without a deal at this point, so Joe Moss unselfishly stumped up the necessary £225 for the studio time. When Morrissey declared himself unhappy with the vocal, Moss stepped in again to pay for it to be re-recorded.[172] The wonderful wailing harmonica intro was a premeditated nod to the similar riff on The Beatles' debut 'Love Me Do' – a deliberate signifier that both records were 'from the mist of the North and from somewhere in the past [but] sounded like the future too' as Marr would later put it.[173] Lyrically, it definitely pointed the way to one aspect of the band that

[171] In *A Light That Never Goes Out*, his marvellously thorough biography of the band, Tony Fletcher also posits the interesting idea that The Smiths' lack of a dues–paying fallow period was the reason they never developed the 'we're-all-in-it-together' attitude that leads most bands to decide on an equal split of the profits.

[172] EMI had already bankrolled demo recordings of 'What Difference Does It Make?', 'Handsome Devil' and 'Miserable Lie' but they passed on signing the band, ironically as it turned out, as they ended up signing them just before they split up.

[173] 'Hand In Glove' was literally from the mists of the North – Stockport was swathed in thick fog the day the song was recorded.

would prove massively significant in the future. It signalled that the uneven band dynamic, which eventually exploded into a ruinous court case, was there from day one. Only two people can be said to be 'Hand In Glove' – clearly the special relationship that's celebrated therein is strictly between Morrissey and Marr. When it comes to lyrical approbation, 'Hand In Glove' doesn't even give Rourke and Joyce the 10% Morrissey thought they deserved. Which is a shame, because Rourke's bass line is the most melodic thing about the song and subsequently mixed significantly higher than the guitars. Despite this slightly unbalanced production, it's clearly a brilliant recording and the band were understandably determined to get it released.

The Saturday after it was completed, Johnny took a cassette of 'Hand In Glove' to the Rough Trade shop in London's Notting Hill. He somehow managed to secure a tête-à-tête with label boss Geoff Travis, who promised to listen to it over the weekend. On top of his songwriting and guitar playing, Johnny's personality was a massive part of The Smiths' success. The Fall were signed to Rough Trade for the best part of three years while I occupied the drum stool and I never had a one-to-one conversation with Travis at any point, despite the fact he co-produced two of our singles. In fact no one at Rough Trade ever really knew who I was, but the Monday morning after he dropped off that cassette everyone who worked there was aware of Johnny Marr. This was far from unique to Rough Trade of course. Me, Johnny and Jim Glennie of James are fellow alumni of the venerated Wythenshawe College of Higher Education between 1980 and 1982. It's safe to say everyone knew who Johnny Marr was, while Jim and I managed to remain completely anonymous for the duration. At least Jim had an excuse – James didn't play their first gig until 1982.[174] Ironically, according to Johnny Rogan's *The Severed Alliance*, Marr 'raved over The Fall's "Totally Wired"' at this time. Well he never let it slip in the queue for apple crumble.

The band's cinematographic ascent continued when Travis immediately agreed to put the single out, backed with 'Handsome Devil', a live track taken from their debut at the Haçienda. After just one play of the A-side on his radio show, The Smiths secured a much-coveted John Peel session.

The next stage in the progress of the band came three days after the Peel recording, when Rough Trade secured them a support slot at a major London venue with a prestigious Manchester band who were also signed to the label. On 21st May 1983 they supported The Fall at Camden's Electric Ballroom. The Fall had just returned from the lengthy tour of the USA via Iceland and were about as well drilled and stage ready as we ever were,[175] but The Smiths more than held their own and the evening was an unqualified success, despite a brief backstage altercation between bands about whose beer was whose.[176] It represented another landmark in The Smiths' continuing rapid progress. Much to Mark E. Smith's chagrin, this progress quickly reached the point where they became Rough Trade's number one priority.

---

[174] James recorded their first two EPs *Jimone* and *James II* in August '83 and October '84 at Strawberry – though the five songs were treated to so little EQ they could really have been recorded anywhere. The band chose what that considered to be their least commercial songs for inclusion on the two EPs, and would brook no aural enhancement or studio jiggery-pokery. Factory must have been delighted.

[175] This was Brix's first night doing the lights for The Fall, having arrived from the US only a couple of days before. A quick listen to the recording of The Fall's set reveals the following stage direction from MES – 'Can you dim the lights down, please? Yeah, thanks, a bit hot.' Which contrasts nicely with his comment to the lighting man the previous May: 'You'd better turn those lights down. Turn 'em up again and I'll just break yer fucking neck, right?'

[176] It was theirs.

The Smiths' first attempt at recording their debut album took place in London, at Wapping's Elephant Studios. It was produced by Troy Tate, who had previously played with Fashion and The Teardrop Explodes, and no one was happy with the result. With the clock ticking, Travis cut a deal with Keith Hopwood to re-record the album at Pluto, on the same terms he had negotiated earlier in the year for The Fall. Before they got to work on re-recording the album, they committed 'This Charming Man' to tape as a standalone single at Strawberry. It was deliberately written by Marr as a major-key contrast to the rest of The Smiths' catalogue – and what a contrast it is. Even the dour lyric can't cast a cloud over the chiming guitar's innate sunniness, despite the fact its desolate hillsides and guilty yearnings distil much of the album's less-than-chirpy subject matter. The riff which starts the song stands completely apart from anything The Smiths' contemporaries were coming up with, even Aztec Camera, who Johnny was trying to imitate when he created it. You'd have to go back to Bert Jansch or The Incredible String Band to find such agreeable arpeggiating, and the bass line is scarcely less inventive than the guitar. The way they meld together, mixing funk, folk, rock and pop into something entirely original and yet still completely unforced and convincing is a genuine thrill. Musicians as capable as this rarely wear their talent so lightly, more's the pity.

The Pluto recording, this time with John Porter in the producer's chair, was initially completely congenial. Then the topic of conversation on one of Morrissey and Marr's morning constitutionals from Piccadilly to Pluto hit on the soon-to-be thorny topic of division of profits. That initially innocent discussion would eventually have massive repercussions, as we know, but one of the immediate consequences as far as the album was concerned was that Morrissey buggered off to London and refused to return until Marr had sorted it out. What's more, he only communicated this instruction through Geoff Travis, who regarded Andy Rourke and Mike Joyce as more or less surplus to requirements.[177] No one has ever offered a satisfactory explanation as to why Joe Moss was not involved in any of this when as band manager he would appear to have been perfectly placed to broker an agreement. Who knows – he might even have brought a pen.

Depending on who you believe, either a tacit agreement was reached between Marr, Rourke and Joyce or the subject was never even brought up and recording continued. But it was far from resolved, and whether the unprecedented 40/40/10/10 split was ever verbally settled during the band's lifetime remains a matter of conjecture for those who weren't there. But the lesson remains that if you're going to put a structure in place that flies in the face of all accepted practice *and* the Partnership Act of 1890,[178] you'd better write it down.

The basic recording was completed fairly quickly, as first albums often are, and the bass and drums were committed to tape in short order. Naturally, several days were devoted to the creation of Johnny Marr's multi-layered 'Guitarchestra'. Vocals, for the most part, were not recorded in Manchester. In fact, despite the fact that he had earlier dismissed the possibility to *Melody Maker*, Morrissey moved to the capital as soon as he had enough money to do so, like many a sixties

---

[177] Around the same time, Geoff also tried to convince Mark E. Smith that working with session players rather than a paid band would be a more lucrative business model. While that's probably true, it fails to factor in the difficulties the average session musician might face working with an arranger for whom 'Play it like a snake' represents one of his clearer instructions.

[178] Paragraph 24, subsection 1: 'All the partners are entitled to share equally in the capital and profits of the business.'

beat-group star before him. He later celebrated his relocation to London in the song of the same name.

Probably because its genesis was so unsatisfactorily chaotic, The Smiths' debut doesn't quite come across as the cogent body of work that many other freshman efforts do. Which is a shame, because if it's possible for an album to be refreshingly downbeat, then *The Smiths* is a fine example.

The first track, 'Reel Around The Fountain', arrives as a statement of intent. There's been plenty written about how different from the other Manchester singers Morrissey's world-weary vocal stylings were, but coming after the self-taught simplicity of Buzzcocks, The Fall and Joy Division, Marr and Rourke's sheer musicality seems like revolution. They discarded the strictures of the punk orthodoxy at a stroke. 'Reel Around The Fountain' features a searing Hammond organ and a tinkling grand piano, played by none other than Paul Carrack,[179] that could have been lifted from Dylan's *Highway 61 Revisited* or the Faces' *A Nod's As Good As A Wink... To A Blind Horse*. Only Mike Joyce's drums, in their obvious debt to Buzzcocks' John Maher, provide a link to standard new wave practices. In an attempt to underline this important connection, the drums are unusually high in the mix throughout the album. This was despite the fact that both Morrissey and Geoff Travis had previously expressed reservations about Joyce's ability. However, it's obvious to anyone with half an ear for music that Joyce's restrained playing was the runway that allowed Marr and Rourke to take flight so effortlessly. Joyce was the perfect drummer for The Smiths, and it's to Travis's discredit that he couldn't hear it. In any case, as Joyce's confidence grew, his contributions would

[179] Carrack had previously played and sang with Ace and Squeeze and would go on to join Mike & the Mechanics.

later be the highlights of songs like 'Shakespeare's Sister' and 'The Queen Is Dead'.

Lyrically the song contains many of the Morrissey-by-numbers influences that populate his early songs: there's Shelagh Delaney, of course,[180] but bizarrely he also quotes from not one but two feminist dissertations on the role of women in cinema: Marjorie Rosen's *Popcorn Venus*[181] and Molly Haskell's *From Reverence To Rape*.[182] Few of the band's contemporaries were mining either of those obscure tomes for lyrical inspiration. An article in *The Sun* newspaper, containing spurious accusations regarding 'Handsome Devil's link to paedophilia,[183] meant that the mere mention of the word 'child' in the lyric of 'Reel Around The Fountain' was enough to scupper it as a contender for a single. It was far too soporific anyway.

'You've Got Everything Now' (another Delaney reference) is relatively slight and much more sparsely arranged than its predecessor; it's only obvious use of studio trickery is the ear-catching organ swell into the chorus. As in many a Morrissey lyric, something not quite mentionable is going on in the back of a car.[184]

'Miserable Lie' contains the album's first explicit reference to Manchester – 'What do we get for our trouble and pain?

[180] 'I dreamt about you last night, and I fell out of bed twice' from *A Taste of Honey*.

[181] The title, from a description of the classic scene from Fellini's *La Dolce Vita*.

[182] 'Pin and mount [me] like a butterfly', describing Terence Stamp's *The Collector*.

[183] Appearing on 25th August under the headline '"BAN CHILD-SEX SONG" PLEA TO BEEB' the ham-fisted article claimed that 'Handsome Devil' contained 'clear references to picking up kids for sexual kicks', an allegation it backed up by quoting a line from 'The Hand That Rocks The Cradle'. It also featured a patently made-up quote as Morrissey's response to the allegation: 'I don't feel immoral singing about molesting children.' Thank God *The Sun* doesn't do stuff like that anymore.

[184] E.g. 'This Charming Man', 'That Joke Isn't Funny Anymore' and 'There Is A Light That Never Goes Out'.

Whalley Range!' – and its warm lyric makes it one of the more human and somehow more likeable, as opposed to admirable, songs on the album. Unfortunately, its awkward time shift, which had such an amazing impact live, is a little clumsily rendered on the record.

'Pretty Girls Make Graves' is much more successful, its time signature change far more convincing than the one on the previous track. The bass and drums carry the song almost completely and are consequently mixed far louder than the guitars, until the rather beautiful coda at the end. Lyrically the song resembles nothing so much as the strangulated protestations of one of Kenneth Williams's characters when the subject of sexual advances comes up in the *Carry On* films.[185]

One of the first songs that Morrissey & Marr wrote, 'The Hand That Rocks The Cradle' was originally based on Patti Smith's 'Kimberley'. Smith was an essential touchstone for the nascent duo's compositions and the debt is clear in this song, though Andy Rourke's marvellously ambient bass line does its best to disguise it. The lyric is, at the very least, open to misinterpretation, and if *The Sun* had employed writers with a slightly more literary ear (as if!) or even read Morrissey's lyrics for themselves rather than crib them from a *Sounds* live review, they could have had a field day with some of the phrases therein. Whatever the song is actually about, the way the music echoes the unspoken creepiness of the lyric is indicative of just how good a writer Marr already was when he met Morrissey.

The title of 'Still Ill' is pretty much Morrissey's mission statement in two words. Its lyric sees Morrissey once

[185] Particularly the scene in Hattie Jacques' bedroom (Hattie plays Matron, of course) in *Carry on Doctor*. Cf. 'I'm not that kind of doctor' with 'I'm not the man you think I am'.

again contemplating his 'otherness' and the loneliness and depression that results. These were unusual themes for pop lyrics, especially then, and connected with a swathe of disenfranchised young people who had never had a spokesman before. They became fiercely devoted to the band and took Morrissey to their hearts, where for many he remains to this day. Musically the song bounces along quite happily on top of more of Marr and Rourke's delightful duelling riffage.

It's obvious that far more care and attention were lavished on the recording of the album's single 'What Difference Does It Make?' than many of the other tracks, and it went on to enjoy justified status as a classic. It was probably tagged as a 45 before it was even recorded, which is not really surprising, as you'd have to be remarkably cloth-eared not to recognise the chart potential of 'What Difference Does It Make?'. Its brilliant guitar intro is more straightforward than the one at the start of 'This Charming Man', and probably even catchier as a result. The song's simple A-B-C structure is cleverly enhanced by a gradual build-up of overdubbed guitars and effects to achieve a massive crescendo.[186] This erudite use of Pluto's capabilities elevates the album version from the version recorded for John Peel in September, which just arrives and then departs. In *Autobiography* Morrissey claims he wanted 'Pretty Girls Make Graves' as the third single, which is clearly far less commercial than 'What Difference Does It Make?', and more importantly has a title that would surely never have been allowed anywhere near the charts. It's possible he is being disingenuous, if you could believe him capable of such a thing.

'I Don't Owe You Anything's distinctly sixties vibe is highlighted by more keyboards from Paul Carrack, who uses both Hammond and Fender Rhodes to brilliant effect.

[186] By the end of the song there are 16 layers of guitar.

Morrissey described its production as a 'squashy and spongy Spandau Ballet cuddle-up' but if there's anything that's reminiscent of Messrs Hadley and co it's those guitar chops, which are identical to the ones on 'True'. Johnny Marr would no doubt point out that they're both ripped off from 'Walk On By', which is the song he had in mind when he wrote it. The vocal melody line is reminiscent of Rod McKuen's 'The Lovers'[187] and shares its aching quality, though not its icy detachment. In fact both the lyric and the song itself have a sheen of sentimentality which runs refreshingly counter to the rest of the album. The ritual of 'going out tonight' retains the iconic allure it has in 'This Charming Man' and this time the narrator is up for it, presumably having found something to wear. Unfortunately, the person he's singing to fancies a night in. The song is so hauntingly romantic that on one occasion it brought Mike Joyce close to tears. All in all it was a perfect fit for Sandie Shaw, who recorded it as the B-side of 'Hand In Glove', which though a catchier song didn't suit her half as well.

In Manchester, then as now, the unspeakable crimes of Ian Brady and Myra Hindley were very much the elephant in the room. 'The Moors Murders cast a great shadow over the heart of the city, and Manchester would never be the same' as Dave Haslam put it. In many ways these despicable acts pervade the Manchester atmosphere like the rain. They're present in the melancholic gloom that makes *Unknown Pleasures* so atmospheric and they helped transform 'Bankrobber' from a skank to sad shuffle. Even Neil Sedaka felt it. Though it's fading now, for a time nearly everyone in Manchester could claim some kind of association with the people or

[187] McKuen was an American singer-songwriter known for his translations of Jacques Brel numbers, the most famous of which was 'Seasons In The Sun'. 'The Lovers' was later covered by the Arctic Monkeys.

locales of the Moors Murders story. For those of us of The Smiths' generation, the connection was one of 'there but for the grace of God...', and for many the thought of what had taken place in familiar locations was almost too much to bear. 'Manchester, so much to answer for' indeed.

Clearly Herman's Hermits or The Mindbenders were never going to tackle such a sickening subject, but 10cc had a song about plane bombings,[188] and Mark E. Smith and Ian Curtis were evidently not averse to discussing the evil that men do.[189] None were willing, or more probably able, to broach the subject of Brady and Hindley. But 'Suffer Little Children' was the second song Morrissey and Marr wrote. Morrissey most likely proffered the lyric as a test to see how Marr would react, and Marr more than rose to the challenge. When asked to consider the fact that he and his writing partner had just written the hitherto unwriteable, Marr deliberately invoked the phrase that Tony Wilson used to describe the Manchester mind-set – 'We do things differently' – and if a Manchester band had to tackle this subject sooner or later, The Smiths were the perfect candidates. It's hard to imagine anyone else penning a lyric like it, or anyone scoring so wretched a topic as tastefully or appropriately. It might be the best song on the album, but 'Suffer Little Children' remains a phenomenally hard listen, and no song has ever been more appositely described as 'haunting'. As eminent rock writer Jon Savage has noted, 'Suffer Little Children' was an important moment for Manchester music:

'It's an incredibly sensitive subject and one that I almost feel [Morrissey] was compelled to confront. I mean, it was

---

[188] 'Clockwork Creep'.

[189] Both had touched on the horrors of Nazi death camps, Smith in 'Various Times' and Curtis in 'No Love Lost'.

such a stain on the city, it was as if the sixties ended right then and there in Manchester. Morrissey grew up in the shadow cast by Brady and Hindley, and there's perhaps an unhealthy morbid fascination there, but there's also the sense of an artist wanting to get to grips with the dark side of his city. Whatever the impulse was, it was not shallow nor merely provocative.'

The Smiths were justifiably proud of the song, and made it the B-side of 'Heaven Knows I'm Miserable Now'. This brought it to the attention of the press, and the subsequent furore was deftly handled by Rough Trade's Scott Piering. He organised both a sensitive press statement and a meeting between Morrissey and Ann West, mother of Moors victim Lesley-Ann. In person Morrissey was, of course, able to articulate that his real intentions were honourable and she gave both her blessing and public support to the song. And luckily for the band no one at *The Sun* had the idea of falsifying a link from 'Suffer Little Children' to the earlier outrage about 'Handsome Devil's lyrical intentions.

The Smiths' debut album's main achievement was acting as a signal of just how good the band were going to be. Though it was far from a failure, it was probably more of a work-in-progress than many first albums, and not as satisfactory as it might have been had it enjoyed a more realistic gestation period. In many ways the band were victims of their own chutzpah – they had hustled themselves into the position where their first album was eagerly anticipated before they were ready to deliver it. While it's always unfair to compare a group to The Beatles, it's a mark of how important, and how good The Smiths were that they can bear the weight of the comparison. Both bands boasted a preternaturally dazzling songwriting partnership, and both are instantly defined by the four members who make up their classic line-ups. But by the time The Beatles came to make their first album they had an unprecedented wealth of live experience, and had spent years writing and working together to bring out the best in each other. The Smiths had a way to go before they could say the same.

Where There's Life There's Gotta Be Hope

The Stone Roses

So Young

The Stone Roses

If you were looking for the perfect way to complete the meandering daisy chain that is this story of Manchester's first two major recording studios, you really couldn't do much better. Ian Brown, the music fan who bluffed his way into Keith Hopwood's Pluto studio to hear The Clash record 'Bankrobber', later became the frontman for Manchester legends The Stone Roses. The Roses were one of the last bands of note to work at Strawberry; they recorded their first single with none other than Martin Hannett, the genius producer of *Unknown Pleasures*. With added poignancy, this happened just as the writing was on the wall for studios like Strawberry and Pluto, as the prices they needed to charge to maintain their buildings and equipment grew increasingly unrealistic in the age of digital recording. All that was needed was for The Stone Roses to record a timeless single to end both Strawberry's and Hannett's brilliant careers on a high. Unfortunately, whatever 'So Young' is, it's not quite the classic single this story's *denouement* deserves. But it was a significant enough event that in 2007, when Strawberry was awarded a blue plaque by English Heritage, the Roses got their name on it, while for some reason Joy Division didn't.[190]

By 1985, when The Stone Roses and Hannett recorded the single, Strawberry's empire was beginning to contract. At its height it had included Strawberry South, a pressing

[190] The original blue plaque name-checked Paul McCartney (for producing his brother Mike's eponymous album at Strawberry in 1974), Neil Sedaka, 'Stone Roses' and The Syd Lawrence Orchestra (quite fittingly, as their marvellously recorded big-band albums were a brilliant early advertisement for the studio's potential). A replacement plaque, unveiled in 2016, added Joy Division, Martin Hannett and The Smiths. It also added the missing 'The' to 'Stone Roses'.

plant in London and a budget studio across the road in Stockport. The budget studio, known as 'Strawberry 2', was the first to go. It was taken over by TV producer Nick Turnbull who re-christened it 'Yellow 2' and switched it to digital recording. The change in technology made Yellow 2 much more financially viable and by mid-1984 it was doing so well that New Order chose it over Strawberry to record 'Shellshock' for the soundtrack to *Pretty In Pink*. Though the initial recording for 'So Young' began at Yellow 2, Hannett was still convinced of Strawberry's unique advantages, and insisted on returning to the site of his greatest triumphs.

As a record, 'So Young' was an unsatisfying alliance between a band that were a long way from reaching their full potential and a producer who was just about to pass his best.[191] Hannett's relations with Factory were at their worst point when he worked with The Stone Roses, who themselves enjoyed a mutually hostile relationship with Manchester's flagship label. Hannett had sued Factory over unpaid royalties and publically despaired over the way Tony Wilson and co ran their business. What upset him most was Factory prioritising a nightclub over the actual business of making records. Factory, he felt, had become a vehicle for 'a few people who manage to crawl up Tony's arse at the bar in his club'. Wilson, of course, responded to Hannett's dejection with typical insouciance by giving the lawsuit its own FAC catalogue number.

For the Roses, who were keen to play up their status as outsiders, Hannett's estrangement from Wilson was a major

[191] The production on *Bummed*, Happy Mondays' second album, is probably Hannett's last great work. The basic recording was done at Slaughterhouse Studios in Yorkshire but, by the time it came to be mixed, relations between Factory and Hannett had thawed sufficiently for them to engage him. Of course he insisted on Strawberry, and Hannett 'played' the studio's desk and effects like another member of the band. If there's any record where you can hear where the songs were mixed, *Bummed* is it.

plus point. Their manager, Howard Jones, had used his own resignation from Factory and his oath to set up a new label with Hannett to rival it, as his main selling point when signing the band. The Roses weren't interested in the production on *Unknown Pleasures*, they wanted the man who produced 'Cranked Up Really High' by Wythenshawe legends Slaughter and The Dogs. Like many Manchester artists, the Roses had an oedipal relationship with their musical predecessors. They 'gave the impression of being beholden to no one', as Dave Haslam put it, while simultaneously absorbing and adapting the Manchester sound of their youth. This much was obvious, because for their next single they turned to another leading light of the Manchester scene, Peter Hook. Their attitude to Strawberry was equally dichotomous, sneering at its out-of-date décor while recognising that it was still one of the very few 24-track studios that existed outside of both London and record company control.

One aspect of the recording of 'So Young' that has entered Manchester folklore, though wrongly ascribed to Joy Division, is Hannett's insistence that the drums be set up in the roof, which resulted in Reni being stuck up there for two hours after he'd laid down his tracks. He could probably have done with someone up there with him, if only to tell him to calm down a bit. The location was fitting in some ways, as Reni's playing at this time was at least head and shoulders above the rest of the band. In truth he was too proficient for his own good, and consequently the drums completely overpowered the rest of the track.

Though descriptions of the band's sound at this time routinely describe them as 'goth', they weren't really, although Brown's phrasing often contained traces of goth melodrama. 'So Young' actually sounds like it would fit right in at The

Ritz on a Monday night, nestled between 'Do You Believe In The Westworld' by Theatre of Hate and 'Temple Of Love' by The Sisters of Mercy.[192] The Stone Roses' first live review in the *NME*, which was not in any way intended to be complimentary, so succinctly summed them up that the band used it in an advert in the same paper: 'The angst-ridden vocal penetrates the plethora of deranged drumming and screaming feedback.' If you're looking for a one line precis of the single, you couldn't do much better than that.

The record, according to Ian Brown, sounds 'like four lads trying to get out of Manchester'. It was only when they realised that it was a mistake to try and leave their roots behind that they began to produce a coherent noise. Of course, 'So Young' couldn't properly be described as a song, but then neither could 'Fools Gold'. The single's B-side, 'Tell Me', isn't really a song either, but it's a better piece of music than 'So Young', with much better dynamics. It would probably claim a place amongst the Roses better-loved songs if it wasn't ruined by Ian's wobbly Kirk Brandon impression on the vocals. It's also got one of those rock and roll endings that just about work live but sound ridiculous in a studio context. The single wasn't a great debut, all in all, and was largely ignored outside of Manchester when it was released in August 1985.[193] Not that their star shone particularly brightly in Manchester either – the main thing most people knew about The Stone Roses at the time was that their name was spray-painted on an annoyingly large number of Manchester landmarks.

---

[192] The Ritz on Whitworth Street has been one of Manchester's leading dancehalls since 1927. In the eighties it hosted a massively popular post-punk night every Monday, where the one pound entrance fee included a free bottle of Holsten Pils. Bargain.

[193] On the same day as Happy Mondays' first release 'Forty Five'.

In retrospect it was a good thing that the band didn't become known for 'So Young', as it meant that they had the time and space to fully refine their sound and their line-up before being thrust into the national spotlight.

Though only 'So Young' and its B-side were officially released from their time at Strawberry, they recorded some 14 songs for what was intended to be their first album. They realised soon after they'd finished recording that the tracks were nowhere near good enough. The songs eventually saw the light of day as the unofficial album *Garage Flower* in 1996. Of these recordings, the stand out track by far was 'I Wanna Be Adored', which was written on the spot in the studio at the behest of Martin Hannett. It's little exaggeration to say that when you listen to the Strawberry recording of 'I Wanna Be Adored' you're actually hearing the birth of the real Stone Roses. Though this version is nowhere near as polished as John Leckie's immaculate production for their first album proper, the song has a clarity and breathing space that's signally missing from most of their previous efforts. Second guitarist Andy Couzens was deputising for AWOL bassist Pete Garner[194] and the absence of rhythm guitar really allows the song to take flight. What Hannett gave the band more than anything else was showing them, as he had done previously for Joy Division, the power of emptiness. Like the cut-outs on the original sleeve of 'Blue Monday', the real value is in what isn't there.[195]

[194] Garner was astute enough to realise his shortcomings as a bass player were holding the band back and soon did the noble thing, in exactly the same way as Alan Wrigley had done with Herman's Hermits way back in 1963.

[195] Another of the many legends that waft around Factory Records, the idea that the label lost money on every copy of 'Blue Monday' they sold has more than a whiff of urban myth about it. Even if the original sleeve design was so expensive it wiped out all other profits, which is unlikely, the cut-outs were dropped very early in the single's production. So early, in fact, that Peter Saville's personal copy doesn't have them.

The Stone Roses never looked back. What Andrew Collins wrote of the band some years later, 'Geography met Art and Culture, and made History', could equally be applied to Strawberry Studios.

★

On 5th March 1986, Strawberry was sold to Yellow 2. Eric Stewart and Graham Gouldman hadn't recorded there since the early eighties, and Peter Tattersall could only resist the rise of new technology for so long. Yellow 2 owner Nick Turnbull's master plan was to marry the old studio's reputation and name to Yellow 2's cheaper digital recording. Which was, of course, a pretty similar plan to the one Strawberry had when they opened Strawberry 2 in the first place. Within two years he sold the Yellow 2 premises as he realised that having two studios meant he was competing with himself for business. While this downsizing provided some initial bounce back, it became increasingly difficult to keep pace with advances in technology, and Turnbull had nothing like the massive personal attachment to the Strawberry brand his predecessors had. As Strawberry engineer John Pennington put it, 'The industry kind of withdrew to London and [...] Strawberry got left behind.' In a bid to keep afloat, the owners decided to concentrate on video production, but in 1993 Strawberry shut its doors for the last time.

It was a real loss. As well as the seminal records discussed here, Strawberry played host to pretty much all of the significant Manchester acts that appeared during its tenure. It was a second home to Oldham's prog superstars Barclay James Harvest; James made their first records there, The Fall, Simply Red and The Charlatans all spent time within its walls, and from *Unknown Pleasures* onwards the studio was virtually synonymous with Factory Records' output.

The year before Strawberry changed hands, eight miles up the A6, Keith Hopwood had also seen the writing on the wall. Pluto was still doing well enough – Buzzcocks made their final recordings there before they split[196] – and as well as commercials, Hopwood was also composing and recording soundtracks to many of Cosgrove Hall's animated features.[197] These included *The BFG* and *The Wind in the Willows*, which won both a BAFTA and an Emmy. But when Hopwood's partner Malcolm Rowe decided to retire to Anglesey, the company broke up and Hopwood was faced with the prospect of finding new premises on his own. It was obvious that a 5,000 square foot studio right in the centre of Manchester was no longer a viable business model. In 1985, he moved his family out to Tarporley and set up Pluto's third iteration – a studio that he could use for his own soundtrack recording, where he continues to compose and record to this day. Though not as widely celebrated as Strawberry, in its own unassuming way Pluto made a massive contribution to Manchester's recording legacy. Just as its founder had been in his days as one of Herman's Hermits, Pluto was content to let others hog the limelight while it quietly got on with the job in hand.

With that, Manchester's first two professional studios were gone. Though a number of noted studios have come and gone

---

[196] 'I Look Alone' would later see the day as part of *Product*, a 5-album package which collected everything they'd released during their first incarnation.

[197] Cosgrove Hall was a Chorlton-cum-Hardy based animation company run by two graduates of the Manchester College of Art & Design: Brian Cosgrove and Mark Hall. For 30 years they produced brilliant children's animations and at one time provided employment for two seminal Manchester guitarists with an eye for graphic design: Bernard Sumner and John Squire.

in and around Manchester since they first opened their doors, none have achieved quite the same cultural significance. Thanks to the legacy of Strawberry and Pluto, Manchester has seen more of its finest artists record on home soil than any other city in the UK. Apart, of course, from London.

By 1992, Factory was gone as well. It may have ended in failure but, as has been noted many times, what a glorious failure it was. In typical Factory fashion, its two most ridiculous decisions were also its greatest achievements. From the start it was clear that giving bands half of the money and all of the rights meant that any downturn in financial fortune would inevitably lead to the label's doom. And in opening the Haçienda instead of investing in the label, Factory sowed the seeds of its own financial decline. You can only run a club which attracts both hordes of punters who aren't drinking and a massive criminal element for so long, and Factory declared bankruptcy in November 1992. With poignant symbolism, New Order signed to London Records. The Haçienda closed its doors for the final time in 1997.

Burnage-born Oasis sold truckloads of records in the nineties and are arguably Manchester's biggest band of all time, despite the fact they never enjoyed the success in the US that Herman's Hermits, The Hollies or even Freddie and the Dreamers did. Their blend of The Stone Roses' Manc attitude with clever pop that borrowed liberally from its finest practitioners was exactly what the record-buying public wanted. Noel and Liam were also an interviewer's dream, they both had bucketloads of personality and nothing that even resembled an off button. Most importantly of all, they had the nous to never stray too far from the sonic template that made them big, and they were subsequently rewarded with an eye-watering volume of sales. But though they realised their Manchester origins were what set them apart from the rest of their Britpop contemporaries, they also realised that their careers would best be served by basing themselves in the centre of the action. While simultaneously playing up their Man City loving Northern charm to the level of caricature, the Gallagher brothers decamped down south as soon as they (or more probably their record company) could afford it. They even boasted as much on the cover of their second album *(What's The Story) Morning Glory?*, which was shot on Berwick Street in Soho.

The record industry was firmly ensconced in the capital once again. London had won. But for a while at least, Strawberry and Pluto showed it was possible to exist, and even be the best, away from the capital.

And what's more, the connective tissue that made it possible means that the story of Manchester music is a story with a plot. Unlike many musical histories, it's not just a litany of facts. The promoters and managers of Kennedy Street inspired and invested in Graham Gouldman, which gave him a unique opportunity to showcase Manchester music on the world stage. They invested in Peter Tattersall and Eric Stewart, and thus made Strawberry Studios possible. Strawberry subsidised and encouraged the studio upstairs, Pluto, to flourish and become a major player in its own right. And having a world-class studio on their doorstep enabled Martin Hannett and New Order to effectively change the face of music altogether. Strawberry's very existence 'lent strength to the instincts of people like Tony Wilson to [...] resist the dominance of London and instead build a creative music scene locally. To do for music what Granada were doing in television,' in the words of Dave Haslam.

For Mancunians, as for the daughters and sons of many Northern towns and cities, rebellion against the typical view of Northerners as cultural underdogs has always been an important driving force. And for many Northerners, expressing pride in your town's individual achievements is similarly imperative. Not least as a means of counterbalancing years of being lumped together as one homogenous 'North' by a massively Londoncentric media.

This was especially important in the sixties, where the UK's countercultural explosion was more often than not presented to the world as either happening in London or 'out there', somewhere vaguely north of Watford gap. In a world where half of the Likely Lads' accents came from no further north than Bingley and fifty per cent of the Liver Birds were distinctly Blackburnian, standing up for your Northern hometown's artistic uniqueness became a way of life.[198]

Of course, lots of Northern towns and cities share that attitude of simultaneous inferiority and superiority that creates and spurs on thriving music scenes, labels and studios. And Manchester doesn't exist in a vacuum. None of the artists discussed here recorded exclusively in Manchester, and many of them don't even live here anymore. And yet... why did such a considerable number of people who saw the Sex Pistols at the Free Trade Hall in 1976 immediately go out and form significant bands of their own? What gave Buzzcocks the idea that they could form their own label, release *Spiral Scratch*, and thus inspire a thousand indie labels? Certainly their self-belief was informed by Northern attitude, and Shelley in particular wore his Northern roots on his sleeve as prominently as his

[198] TV's willingness to present the North as one interchangeable location continued way past the sixties of course. It always amazed me that in Carla Lane's risible 'comedy' *Bread* the distinctly Scouse Boswells boasted a middle son with a Manchester accent.

heart. But it wouldn't have happened without the do-it-yourself and do-it-away-from-London legacy of Kennedy Street, The Mindbenders, Herman's Hermits and Graham Gouldman. One of the reasons the Manchester scene of 1977 was so richly rewarding was because the protagonists were standing on the shoulders of giants.[199]

If this Manchester attitude has been passed from generation to generation, is the 'Manchester sound' similarly bequeathed? Can a Manchester sound even exist, when what we think of Manchester music runs the gamut of emotions from 'I'm Into Something Good' to 'I Remember Nothing'?

The simple answer is yes, when Morrissey can make a Graham Gouldman/Herman's Hermits song like 'East West' feel like he wrote it himself, or when the same unnamed introspection haunts both 'I'm Not In Love' and 'Thieves Like Us'. The palpable tinge of regret that colours the palette of L.S Lowry also colours much of the region's music, from 'East West' to 'Charlemagne'[200] via 'Blue Monday' and 'Sad Sweet Dreamer'.[201] It flows like a river through Elbow's elegiac back catalogue[202] and was sufficiently palpable to alter the perspective of visiting artists as diverse as Neil Sedaka and The Clash, and it's probably the reason there's never been a decent heavy metal band from Manchester – little room for melancholy there.

One of the main ironies about the fact that The Stone Roses recorded and mixed 'So Young' just as the sun was

[199] Note the plural. It's not possible to stand on the 'Shoulder of Giants', Noel.

[200] A hit in 2015 for Stockport's Blossoms. What a shame they never got to record it at Strawberry.

[201] A No. 1 in 1974 for Sweet Sensation. Golden-voiced lead singer Marcel King later recorded for Factory but died at the tragically young age of 37 in 1995.

[202] Elbow managed to buck the prevailing trend by recording most of their material at Salford's Blueprint Studios.

setting on Strawberry Studios was the song's subject matter. It was written as a repudiation of the elegiac nature of many Manchester bands, in particular The Smiths. Unlike their immediate predecessors, The Stone Roses had little time for the city's predilection for songs of sorrowful introspection, and they had no desire to continue the tradition. They associated Manchester bands with 'misery, shyness and depression' according to bassist Pete Garner, and 'it didn't seem right to us'. In the lyric for 'So Young', as he leafs through a metaphorical list of Manchester groups from The Hollies to The Smiths, Ian Brown makes it clear he's less than impressed: 'In the misery dictionary, page after page after page.'

But we can forgive him because, as he admitted in the title, he was only young. Branding a tendency for thoughtfulness and introspection as 'miserable' is a mistake, even in reference to a band with a real reason to be miserable like Joy Division. And Ian Brown, with the wisdom of years, would no doubt acknowledge that now, because Manchester's propensity for slightly darker hews is actually what allowed many of its best artists to achieve greater depth of feeling, including The Stone Roses themselves. And surely a degree of depth can be no bad thing in a world where shallowness seems to be celebrated more and more. What's more, far from being miserable, the malcontents and moaners who refused to bend the knee to a London-based industry eventually conceived and nurtured a glorious catalogue of recorded music.

In 1929, as they sang 'Nymphs And Shepherds' into Columbia's primitive microphones, the Manchester Children's Choir urged the people of Manchester to 'express your jollity'. They may not have quite got the mood right but they were right about one thing: Manchester will forever be a place whose very essence is filled 'with music, with dancing and with poetry'.

By the way, I hope that in celebrating Manchester's place in the history of recorded British music, I've expressed justifiable pride in the achievements of my hometown without the xenophobic undertones that often accompany pride in the achievements of one's country. A distinct distaste for that brand of flag-waving is why I always feel more comfortable supporting Manchester United than England. For most of us, the rivalry between Manchester and Liverpool, for instance, can be celebrated and enjoyed because it doesn't come with the extra baggage of an assumed superiority. Though Manchester is clearly better.

Bibliography

Bangs, L, in DeCurtis, A (ed): *The Rolling Stone Illustrated History of Rock & Roll: The Definitive History of the Most Important Artists and Their Music* Random House 1992

Blacknell, S and Humphries, P: *Top of the Pops: 50th Anniversary* McNidder & Grace 2013

Diggle, S: *The Buzzcocks: Harmony In My Head – Steve Diggle's Rock 'n' Roll Odyssey* Helter Skelter 2003

Fletcher, T: *The Clash: The Complete Guide To Their Music* Omnibus Press 2005

Fletcher, T: *A Light That Never Goes Out* Random House 2012

Ford, S: *Hip Priest: The Story of Mark E Smith and The Fall* Quartet Books 2013

Gatenby, P and Gill, C: *The Manchester Music History Tour* Empire Publications 2011

Goddard, S: *Mozipedia: The Encyclopaedia of Morrissey and The Smiths* Ebury Press 2012

Green, J with Barker, G: *A Riot of Our Own: Night and Day with The Clash* Orion 2003

Hanley, S and Piekarski, O: *The Big Midweek: Life Inside The Fall* Route 2016

Haslam, D: *Manchester, England: The Story of the Pop Cult City* Fourth Estate 2000

Hook, P: *Unknown Pleasures: Inside Joy Division* Simon & Schuster 2013

Lawson, A: *It Happened in Manchester* Multimedia 1990

Lee, CP: *Shake Rattle and Rain – Popular Music Making in Manchester 1955 – 1995* Hardinge Simpole 2002

Lewisohn, M: *The Beatles – All These Years: Volume One: Tune In* Little Brown 2015

MacDonald, I: *Revolution In The Head: The Beatles Records and the Sixties* Pimlico 1998

McGartland, T: *Buzzcocks The Complete History* Music Press Books 2017

Marr, J: *Set The Boy Free* Century 2016

Massey, H: *The Great British Recording Studio* Hal Leonard Corporation 2015

Morley, P: *Joy Division: Piece by Piece* Plexus Publishing Ltd 2007

Morrissey, S: *Autobiography* Penguin Classics 2013

Nolan, D: *I Swear I Was There: Sex Pistols, Manchester, and the Gig That Changed the World* Music Press Books 2016

Noone, S: *Seekers Guide to the Rhythm of Yesteryear* Cecil Sharp House 2012

Nice, J: *Shadowplayers – The Rise and Fall of Factory Records* Aurum 2010

Robb, J: *Punk Rock: An Oral History* Ebury Press 2006

Robb, J: *The Stone Roses and The Resurrection of British Pop* Ebury Press 2001

Robb, J: *The North Will Rise Again: Manchester Music City 1976-1996* Aurum Press 2010

Rogan, J: *Morrissey & Marr – The Severed Alliance* Omnibus 1992

Salewicz, C: *Redemption Song: The Definitive Biography of Joe Strummer* HarperCollins Entertainment 2007

Southall, B: *The Road is Long: The Hollies Story* Red Planet 2015

Spence, S: *The Stone Roses War and Peace* Viking 2012

Strummer, J; Jones, M; Simonon, P and Headon, N: *The Clash* Atlantic Books 2010

Stewart, E: *The Things I Do For Love* Eric Stewart 2017

Sumner, B: *Chapter and Verse – New Order, Joy Division and Me* Corgi 2015

Topping, K: *The Complete Clash* Reynolds & Hearn 2003

Tremlett, G: *The 10cc Story* Futura 1976

Thompson, D: *10cc – The Cost of Living In Dreams* CreateSpace Independent Publishing Platform 2012

Acknowledgments

Firstly, my thanks to all the amazing musicians and music-people who populate these pages, who have inspired me for years and continue to do so. To Selwyn and Isabel for their belief, support and invaluable advice (and for the posh biscuits – you can't buy class). Special thanks to Harvey Lisberg and Keith Hopwood for their patient recollections. Thanks to Mick Middles and Jon Robb for their encouragement. Thanks to Steve for getting me into yet another fine mess and to him and Olivia for showing me what was possible. To Harry and Jude and Andrew and Harriett for always being there. Massive thanks to Julie, Roseanna, Adam and Nathan for their love and unwavering support and encouragement. Thanks to my brilliant and much-missed parents Pat & Pat (Irish, were they?) not least for getting on a train when they got off the ferry. And finally thanks to Manchester: we strive for perfection and if we fail we might just have to settle for excellence.

Paul Hanley was the drummer in Manchester legends The Fall from 1980-85 and now plays with Brix & The Extricated. He's studying for an English degree with the Open University and occasionally writes for *Louder Than War*. He's married with three children and once got 21 on Ken Bruce's 'PopMaster'.

For more on this book please visit
www.leavethecapital.wordpress.com
www.route-online.com